COLLINS GUIDE
TO WILD HABITATS

GRASSLAND AND SCRUB

A grassland grazer

COLLINS GUIDE TO WILD HABITATS

CHRIS PACKHAM

With 39 colour photographs
by the author and 5 colour
plates by Chris Shields

LEFT **Our ancient land**
RIGHT **Grasses**

COLLINS
Grafton Street

GRASSLAND AND SCRUB

This book is for my parents, who
should never have shown me Mrs
Greenwood's Ladybird bush.

William Collins Sons & Co Ltd
London · Glasgow · Sydney · Auckland
Toronto · Johannesburg
Text and photographs © 1989 Chris Packham
Colour plates © 1989 Chris Shields

First edition 1989

Art Editor: Caroline Hill
Designer: Frances Mckay

ISBN 0 00 219843 6 Paperback
ISBN 0 00 219869 X Hardback
Filmset by Ace Filmsetting Ltd,
Frome, Somerset
Colour origination by
Wace Litho, Birmingham, UK
Printed and bound by
New Interlitho SpA, Milan, Italy

CONTENTS

RIGHT **Hoary Hogweed**

Acknowledgements are due to Peter Merrett and Jeremy Thomas of Furzebrook Research Station; to Chris Haes, for up-to-date cricket scores; to Rory Putman of Southampton University; to Jane Harvey of Canon UK, for loan of photographic equipment; to Ashley Smith and Jim Chick of the Hawk Conservancy at Weyhill; to John Guliver; to Andy Welch and John Buckley, for being Great White Beetle and Bug catchers and for letting me be a Silverfish; to Gerry Mundey, the world's greatest enthusiast; and to Barbara Levy. Special thanks are due to my continually abused parents; to the Prettiest Star, still brighter than Betelgeuse; to the Tiny Twinkle-heart, for glamour and grammar; and to Jenny for burning dogs.

Acknowledgement is definitely not due to Stephen 'Crunchy-Bark-Bark' Bolwell, who fed all of my drafts to his Weasels and later blamed the curse of Barstardos for his own predicaments.

LEFT **A Bee Orchid**

ACKNOWLEDGEMENTS

My mirror was pure azure. I watched the shadows lace up the cockpit and the sun catch the mirror. It turned silver and then melted yellow gold. I pushed the Spitfire's joystick down, twisted its wicked curves seaward and, with the monotonous power of the Merlin engine racking me, I levelled out over the Channel and hammered in to Kent over Sandwich Bay. Here, I managed to dissolve myself from reality. I rolled low over the North Downs, looking down into the deep escarpments that seemed iced with Yew, pricked with Hawthorn and capped with Beech. White sheep wriggled like maggots on a billiard table. A landscape of soft grassland led me low into the great horseshoe of hills that form The Weald. Then for 90 kilometres, I roared over the South Downs, over the Cuckmere, the Ouse, the Adur, and the Arun rivers. On over a short grass prairie spotted with woods and occasional patchworks of tiny fields, all neatly hemmed with soft hedgerows, mixed on a pallet of olives, yellows and a thousand greens, and detailed with myriads of wild flowers, obliterated by my speed. I followed the countryside through Sussex and up into Hampshire, where parts of the land recalled The Weald woodlands. Here, I lifted my Spitfire and, as if cruising along a straight open road at the wheel of an old Bentley, I headed out over Wiltshire, over Stonehenge and onto the vast plain beyond. Vaguely splattered with lumps of Juniper, Hawthorn and Beech, the woodlands here were few and far between. It was all grassland; wide-open, windy and ancient. Banking high over the Marlborough Downs, I retraced my wings down the Avon, bent the spire of the Cathedral at Salisbury and sped on to Martin Down on the Hampshire/Wiltshire border. Feeling the waxy braid tight on my doeskin glove I pulled my joystick back, and looping, watched the world invert. Then, at my favourite place in the whole world, I woke up.

LEFT **Low over the North Downs**
RIGHT **The grass sea**

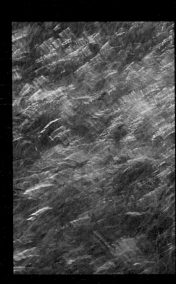

My romantic tirade over southern England had been uncomfortably terminated with a savage dry mouth and a milky, bleached view over the reserve. I had fallen asleep beside a Burnt Orchid, and the only cannons at my fingertips were two rather scratched black cameras and their battered lens barrels. Worse, I hadn't fired a shot all afternoon. In my absence the day had decayed, the sky had turned white and bled a bright light over the land. This crept, with an irritating intensity, into every crack, crevice and crease, whether large or small. It made me squint so hard that my eyes twitched. With a desperate craving for lemonade, I got up and made my way down the bank, my feet falling flat and painfully on the hard, baked and dazzling chalk path. A speck flickered in the skies, and through force of habit I took a tortured look through my binoculars. It was a little Kestrel, burnt to a smoky black silhouette. He rapidly slipped and wheeled sideways, giving me a brief flash of feather detail. A black subterminal band on his fanning tail betrayed his sex, as I wished my pupils would contract more efficiently. He bounced up and again hung from an invisible thread, peering down into the minutiae of the colourful sward below, waiting on a meal. A little further on, a dreary brown Skylark launched out of the grass like a musical rocket fuelled by liquid trilling. The thought of tracing his path into the fluorescent sky was too much to bear. As usual, the Great British Weather was giving me grievous bodily harm.

Further on, the path decayed and disappeared into an island of scrubby old Hawthorns. Here, a Nightingale punctured the afternoon's hum with its throaty chuckles, whistles and rich phrases. I waited in vain for a full burst. He was only playing with a few scales, in preparation for this evening's solo performance. I made my way to the car park, pausing only to look at a few powder blue butterflies and budding orchids. Arriving at my rusty car, surely the perfect antithesis of a Supermarine Spitfire, I turned to look back up the escarpment. A few Rooks blew noisily from right to left, homing rapidly on their homes in the Ash, above a field where I had once watched a party of Stone Curlews displaying on my birthday. A great present which would never be repeated. The scene had none of the greens that I had dreamt of. It was a bland, broken and bleak sea of striated fawns and browns, which threw up occasional wrecks in the form of beaten and straggly Hawthorn bushes. The ridge beyond was tantalisingly distant and all details were lost through the obscene light.

Despite the horror and repulsion I had felt on waking, and my manic quest for refreshment, something jarred. It was not through any political fervour, certainly not through any sense of national patriotism. It was purely based on an aesthetic cohesion with a landscape which had spawned me that I thought, 'This is England'. This cold sea of grass, deserted, aching and dying in a disgusting abuse of agriculture, was England. It was a scar, a wound on 1988 which peeled back to reveal a landscape of yesteryear. I gazed at a view which had waved farewell to the archers who went to Agincourt. I listened to sheep that had bleated behind the Roundheads' revolution and I stroked grass that had brushed the ankles of mares that had charged at Balaclava. That lark had spoken to Rupert Brooke, and somehow, this field was still forever England.

My sentiment for the permanence, the antiquity, the magical aura that this instils and for the simplicity of the commanding escarpments has not been shared by all. Gilpin in 1804 described it as 'disfiguring', Granville in 1841 as 'dismal, barren and discouraging'. Finally, with his usual pompous gusto, Johnson said the South Downs were so desolate that, if he had to live there, he would hang himself – if he could find a tree to fasten the rope to! Clearly this wag was too busy being profound to crouch on his knees and marvel at the outrageous design of a Bee Orchid, or to wonder at the light of Glow-worms. At least Gilbert White, the great naturalist of

Selborne, shared an affinity with a host of botanists, birders, hikers and post-war picnickers. People who can distinguish the smell of downland from sweet heath, musty oak-wood and acrid bog. Essence of chalk enhanced by the aromas of Wild Thyme, Marjoram, calamint and Selfheal.

THE EVOLUTION OF DOWNLAND
The history of downland began a 100 million years ago, when Britain was somewhere in the centre of a land called Laurasia, edged along its eastern flank by a long strip of sea known as the Boreal Ocean, the ancestor of the modern North Sea. At this time the eastern side of Laurasia collapsed and the tides flooded in over a vast area, smothering what is now North Western Europe. This 'Chalk Sea', as it is known by geologists, was a clear, warm and tranquil body of water bordered by a desolate, low lying, arid landscape. These conditions ideally suited a group of phytoplankton, the Haptophyceae; a form of algae which have reinforced calcite (a

form of calcium carbonate) walls to support their structure. When these die and decay their strengthening plates slowly sink and are deposited on the ocean floor. For the next 35 million years, the familiar white chalk, that can be found not only in England but Belgium, northern France, Denmark, East and West Germany, Poland, Russia and parts of the Middle East, accumulated at an incredibly slow rate of about two to four millimetres per century. These component particles have never been fully compacted or cemented together giving the soft, crumbly texture of chalk. The rock is also very porous, giving the chalk its characteristic water holding properties. Towards the end of this Upper Cretaceous period, the era when Dinosaurs died out and the diversity of flowering plants bloomed, earth movements were renewed and about 65 million years ago the chalk sea-bed began to rise above water level. Eventually, Africa, which had been steadily creeping up on Europe, finally collided and caused the formation of

In comes the corn

the Alps. The shock waves from this shunt caused a considerable buckling across southern England and a series of east/west folds were formed. These are the ridges of the North and South Downs, the Chilterns and the Cotswolds. By the end of the ensuing bout of ice ages they were completely covered in an inpenetrable forest of elm and oak.

These woods remained until Roman times, when only the tops of hills had been cleared by the Celts for their primitive fields and hill forts. In the fifth century, the Saxons moved into south east England and began to clear the lowland areas and work the fertile, loamy soils. The Normans, post-1066 and all that, delayed the process of clearing by their anarchic destruction of the Saxons' system, but by the 12th century deforestation had begun in earnest and was to continue throughout the Middle Ages. This facilitated England's greatest medieval industry, the wool trade. By the middle of the 14th century, when the human population of England was about two million, there were over eight million sheep bleating about in the rain, providing cloth for rich and poor. These enormous flocks continued to roam the land and with the wool trade booming, the proportion of pasture rose. At the end of the 19th and beginning of the 20th centuries, when agriculture had slumped, over half the total area of England and Wales was grassland.

Such grasslands fall into two categories. 'Permanent grass' is enclosed, fertilised and frequently sown with commercial mixtures of grass species. Today, this type of land occupies more area than any other in Britain. But, because of the hideous efficiency of modern herbicides, much of it is decidedly boring, being composed of few native grass and herb species. In the past, this land was more than likely arable so, historically speaking, it has no roots. The second category is 'rough grassland'. This is more ancient and may have persisted on unploughable hillsides since the forest was cleared over

1,000 years ago. Unfortunately, since the end of the last war, this rich and valuable habitat has been systematically destroyed. Even through the 1960s the Ministry of Agriculture stubbornly refused to liaise with the then embryonic Nature Conservancy Council, and the ploughing continued unabated. Now, as I write, a local site, consisting of two unexplored ancient monuments and a nationally important Site of Special Scientific Interest (SSSI) stands helpless before an army of bulldozers and warm tarmac. I wish Dr Johnson were here to be profound, as I am sure he would now lament the demise of our downland and not be in such a hurry to find himself a tree!

GRASSES

The coolness, mildness and continual dampness of the British Isles and much of northern Europe ideally fulfils all the growth requirements of one group of plants, the grasses. Our climate is not alone in this characteristic. No other family is more widespread across the globe. The steppes of Asia, the prairies and plains of North America and the savannahs of South America, Africa, and Australia mean that 30 per cent of the surface vegetation of our planet is dominated by the grasses.

Due to their fundamental importance to man since the dawn of agriculture, grasses were recognised as a natural group long before the science of Botany. The domestication of Wheat, Oats and Barley by prehistoric man was a keystone in the foundations for our many civilisations. Today, Rice, Wheat, Millet and Rye form the basis of the daily diet for millions and millions of people. Maize, Barley and other cereals are also used for livestock production, and a mass of other pasture grasses support grazing animals which provide us with meat, milk, butter, hides and wool.

If you have never looked, wander into your garden, or the nearest park, get down on your knees and examine a grass plant. It is easily distinguished from other plant families by its hollow, jointed stem. These joints are known as nodes, and at the base of each is an active growing area which causes the stem to elongate. The leaves are usually alternately spaced up this stem and consist of two parts. The sheath arises at the node and encircles the stem, where it protects the aforementioned delicate and fragile growing zone. The blade separates from the sheath and flops out from the stem to catch the sun and, through the process of photosynthesis, provides the plant with energy.

Grass flowers are normally not brightly coloured or flamboyant, being only a simple assemblage of bracts and cusps which enclose the stamens and stigma. In fact these flowers are so simplified, reduced and regular that they are only of minor importance in grass identification. The spikelets on which clusters of flowers are held are, however, extremely variable and a stroll across a piece of rough land and onto a football pitch will reveal a host of different forms which are often quite attractive. For the amateur the identification of grasses is considerably more difficult than wild flowers. Keys are required to separate many of the species, and this generally requires tiny parts of greenery to be held quivering under a hand lens.

Two species of grass dominate the sward on British downlands. Sheep's Fescue *Festuca ovina* and Red Fescue *F. rubra* occur in almost equal abundance and are superficially very similar, being rather small tufted plants with long bristle-like leaves. Both produce lateral shoots which emerge from the sheath of scales at the base of the tuft and creep over the soil for a short distance. If these shoots, or tillers, escape the chomping of rabbits, or sheep, they produce leaves and then develop into new, erect flowering tufts. If they are constantly grazed or mown, fresh shoots sprout close to the base of the established mother plant. These spread more slowly but it is this network of material together with the mat of fibrous roots that fills the upper ten centimetres of soil and forms the characteristic velvety, springy carpet of downland turf.

Amongst the blanket of fescue which undoubtly forms the largest bulk of the herbage, several other grass species appear. The commonest is Common Oat Grass *Helictofrichon pratense*, which is sometimes joined by Downy Oat-grass *Avenula pubescens*, Yellow Oat-grass *Trisetum flavescens* or False Oat-grass *Arrhenatherum elatius*. Some of these species are quite intolerant of grazing and are more typical of wasteland or roadside verges which are infrequently cut rather than persistently grazed. In the south east of England, Tor Grass *Brachypodium pinnatum* can often be identified by its spreading circular patches which appear light yellow in colour. This species has recently increased, due to the reduction in the number of sheep because, although its leaves are eaten when young and fresh, once the parent plant is mature the foliage becomes dry and unnutritious and is consequently disregarded by the delicate palates of the grazers. Upright Brome *Bromus erectus*, Crested Hair Grass, *Koeleria macrantha* and Quaking Grass *Briza media*, are other species characteristic of poor, dry soils, and they regularly occur on downland. Tall meadow grasses, such as Tufted Hair-grass *Deschampsia cespitosa*, Tall Fescue *F. arundinacea*, the pest Yorkshire Fog *Holcus lanatus*, the ever abundant Common Bent *Agrostis capillaris*, Crested Dogstail *Cynosurus cristatus*, Sweet Vernal Grass *Anthoxanthum odoratum* and Timothy *Phleum pratense* may occur in isolated patches but are never really common because they need excessive humus and damp soils. These requirements are quite untypical of downland where the soil is usually very shallow, often only 25 cm deep. Beneath this lies the chalk bedrock which is very porous, which means that this spartan substrate is also excessively dry. In its favour the soil is rich in calcium, a nutrient essential to many plants, which is leached from the soluble parent rock.

The herbs which occur on downland are characteristically low growing perennials, less than ten per cent being annual or biennial. This imbalance is the result of the intense competition to grow in the dense sward. Gaps in the foliage are so sparse that few species run the risk of needing to re-establish themselves each year. Thirty-five per cent of those herbs that occur here are small, flattened, rosette-like plants which are less likely to be damaged by the continual chomping of herbivores' teeth. When extremely close cropping by rabbits or sheep continues for years there is often a tendency to dwarfing. In the past this has led several plants to be proposed as new and distinct species. In reality, they are no more than tiny, stunted variants of common species. The advantage of their small size is that these plants are able to flower and set seed whilst their giant relations have their heads bitten off by the armies of incisors, something that is especially important for the annuals and biennials.

A foray onto downland in summer is a colourful treat. The compact heads of small, mauvish green flowers and pinnate leaves of the Salad Burnet *Sanguisorba minor* can be found almost everywhere. This is one of many deeply rooted species which probes a metre down so that it can tap supplies of water, even when the surface soil is baked dry in late summer. Small Scabious *Scabiosa columbaria* is another deep rooted plant which is botanically described as a 'calcicol' (calcium loving). Such species habitually occur on alkaline limestone or chalky soils and are unable to survive elsewhere. (Species such as Foxgloves *Digitalis purpurea* are known as 'calcifuges' (calcium hating), because they literally take refuge from limey soils and can only grow under neutral or slightly acid conditions.) The sweet smelling Wild Thyme *Thymus praecox* constantly appears on downland, as does Dwarf Thistle *Cirsium acaule* with its compact rosette of prickly leaves and its single, striking, crimson flower. Fairy Flax *Linum catharticum* with its tiny white flowers, and the Burnet Saxifrage *Pimpinella saxifraga*,

an umbelliferous plant which may grow up to a metre high on ungrazed grassland, join Bird's-foot Trefoil *Lotus corniculatus*, Rough Hawkbit *Leontodon hispidus*, Red Clover *Trifolium pratense* and Ribwort Plantain *Plantago lanceolata* as plants which may occur in moderate abundance on downland but can also be found on other types of grassland. Harebell *Campanula rotundifolia*, Common Knapweed *Centaurea nigra*, Ox-eye Daisy *Leucanthemum vulgare*, Bulbous Buttercup *Ranunculus bulbosus*, Selfheal *Prunella vulgaris*, Lady's Bedstraw *Galium verum* and Cowslip *Primula veris* are not confined to chalk but all add to the splendid splattering of colour in summer. Round-headed Rampion *Phyteuma tenerum* and Little Squinancywort *Asperula cynanchica* which are only found on the chalklands often form dense patches. Dropwort *Filipendula vulgaris*, with its small white flowers and rosy pink buds, and Horseshoe Vetch *Hippocrepis comosa*, with its characteristically equine pods, are both locally common and their flowers may turn the slopes golden during mid-summer. Kidney Vetch *Anthyllis vulneraria*, Carline Thistle *Carlina vulgaris*, Hairy Violet *Viola hirta*, Hedge Bedstraw *Galium mollugo*, Autumn Gentian *Gentianella amarella* and Wild Carrot *Daucus carota* can all be found commonly in this community. The light yellow flowers of the Common Rock-rose *Helianthemum nummularium* open widely over its dark green leaves and sometimes smother areas of very short turf. The beautiful blue-flowered Perennial Flax *Linum perenne* can be found on the chalk of eastern England, where the magnificent purple Pasque Flower *Pulsatilla vulgaris* is now unfortunately a rare species. Common Milkwort *Polygala vulgaris* in its pink-, white- or blue-flowered forms is never uncommon on downland and seems to show a particular affinity for growing on the tops of anthills, molehills or rabbit burrows. To outline all the species which contribute to the vibrant palette of downland turf, all the yellows, the mauves, the blues and the whites, would result in a tedious listing of a large proportion of the British flora. The habitat is incredibly rich, not only botanically, but also in butterflies, beetles and our most unpopular invertebrates the spiders. What better way to begin than to introduce one of our most attractive and unique arachnids.

A GRASSLAND SPIDER

Pisaura mirabilis is a grey-brown spider identified by a thin yellowy-white median line on its carapace, and paler sides to its tapered abdomen. Together the carapace and abdomen measure a little over a centimetre and a half long. Its long legs are similarly coloured, the two pairs of fore-legs being held close together as it moves rapidly through the grass in search of prey. It is easily located from mid-June onwards, by searching for its tent-like nursery web. This is often spun amongst the upper stems of grass tufts growing on overgrown downland or heathland, across much of southern England. A large and obvious affair, up to about 20 centimetres across, the nursery web appears somewhat like a gossamer jellyfish slumbering in the grass. It acts as a protective canopy for the numerous spiderlings which erupt from the spherical egg-sac that the female carries on all her travels. Even after they have hatched, the mother is not relieved of the burden of parenthood because she remains guarding the cluster of youngsters from the outside of the web. However, anybody discovering this pallid marquee will have unfortunately long since missed this species's unique behaviour.

The presentation of a courtship gift by a male to a female during the preliminaries of a sexual encounter is fairly commonplace in many carnivorous species, particularly in birds. Think of the tender trilling made by the tiny male Sparrowhawk hidden in the canopy of a birch tree as he presents a poor, plucked tit to his larger mate; or the silent passing of a silvery minnow in the shade of a jade stream by a male Kingfisher. In spiders, however, only one species in the world performs such behaviour and that is *Pisaura mirabilis.*

Quite why this form of behaviour has developed in this particular species is unknown, but it does serve several important functions. Any courtship is a process designed to incur a level of sexual synchrony between prospective mates. When this is achieved the all important act of copulation can occur. On the male's part, it is a ritual that enables him to identify himself and then pacify his intended mate so he can successfully transfer his sperm. Firstly then, the male *Pisaura* hunts for a prey item, often a small fly. The size of the prey he can handle is related to his size – larger spiders catch larger flies – and once killed the offering is tightly bound in a web of silk. Then it is carried in the chelicerie (jaws) until a female is encountered and after a brief tactile greeting he presents this to her. The male then begins transferring his sperm to the female, which for spiders is an indirect process. Consequently it is a time consuming affair and this is the crux of this behavioural curiosity.

If the male is large then his larger gift will take longer to eat and his chance of successful copulation is increased. If he is small, the female will rapidly devour the prey and his chances are decreased. This process is known as sexual selection. In this case the females actively choose the male on the basis of the size of the meal they supply, and thus larger and fitter males are more likely to get their genes into the next generation. Mating usually occurs just once, because males are only active for a few days and are rapidly predated as they rove about in search of mates. The gift also serves as an immediate source of nourishment, which will help the female produce a larger number of eggs and this again is beneficial to the fitness of the species. What is seemingly such a simple and subtle gesture is in fact a critical survival mechanism driven by evolution. There is so much more to spiders than a shriek at a black blur in a bathtub!

Downland is a habitat which is dependent on the hand of man, or more precisely the appetite of his stock, for its origins and precarious existence. It is not a stable climax community (that is the ecological community that would result if an area was left *completely* alone. In Britain this would be oak or beech woodland), but rather a single early stage of native vegetation that has been jammed in a time-warp for nearly a thousand years. Yet it is very sensitive and any change, from undergrazing to overgrazing, the substitution of sheep by cattle, or even in the time of year when pastures are grazed, will lead to immediate and visible changes in the vegetation. Under a constant regime of grazing, permanent grass communities can attain a considerable stability. But if the teeth stop chomping there is a serious and widespread deterioration of the grassland and a turn towards the establishment of plant communities which are much more commonplace and less unique than true downland. The pasture is rapidly invaded by shrubs and the development to woodland follows fairly rapidly.

Hawthorn *Crataegus monogyna* is the most frequent pioneer scrub-builder. At first there are only scattered clumps with open herbage between but this space is rapidly filled with brambles and roses. Through this closed thicket, Hazel *Corylus avellana*, Dogwood *Cornus sanguinea* and Dwarf Elder *Sambucus nigra* appear, their fruits being rapidly spread by visiting birds who now find perches growing on the previously barren slopes. Spindletree *Euonymus europaeus*, with its beautiful pink fruits, Wild Privet *Ligustrum vulgare*, with its black berries, and the Wayfaring Tree *Viburnum lantana*, with its scarlet fruits and yellow and orange foliage, all provide a bright contrast to the many black berries of the Buckthorn *Rhamnus catharticus*, but whilst they look colourful they are blan-

LEFT **Marbled White on chalk scree**
RIGHT **Dandelions**

17

keting out the groundlayer and the herb flora changes drastically. It is at this stage of scrubland development that that handsome and conspicuous plant Deadly Nightshade *Atropa belladonna*, sprouts its dull purple and green bells. White Bryony *Bryonia cretica*, Honeysuckle *Lonicera periclymessum* and Bittersweet *Solanum dulcamara*, which has flowers like those of potatoes, also all appear. Traveller's-joy, otherwise known as Old Man's Beard, *Clematis vitalba* which cloaks the developing Hawthorns in a cloud of frothy filigree in the bleak days of winter, joins Common Gromwell *Lithospermum officinale*, Wild Liquorice *Astragalus glycyphyllos*, Columbine *Aquilegia vulgaris*, Common Meadow-rue *Thalictrum flavum* and the characteristic Crested Cow-wheat *Melampyrum cristatum* as species which prefer lime rich soils, but only become established with the onset of scrub encroachment. Ploughman's Spikenard *Inula conyza*, Hairy St John's-wort *Hypericum hirsutum*, Marjoram *Origanum vulgare*, Nettle-leaved Bellflower *Campanula trachelium* and Long-stalked Cranesbill *Geranium columbinum* also appear as soon as the sheep and rabbits disappear.

Whitebeam *Sorbus aria* is a characteristic species of a slightly later stage, and with the Field Maple *Acer campestre* and the Box *Buxus sempervirens*, this may persist into the eventual climax which is typically Common Beech *Fagus sylvatica* woodland on chalk. By now the myriads of tiny flowers, including all the rarities, and all the insects they support have long gone and the ground layer is no more than a dark carpet of dead leaves. Despite the many new birds, insects and mammals which appear throughout the development from scrubland to woodland the unique quality of the precious downland habitat has been eroded forever. It is clear that given the chalk bedrock, the thin dry soils it produces and the correct climate, it is grazing which produces downland and in fact only two species are responsible for its maintenance, the sheep and the rabbit.

GRASSLAND GRAZERS

The snub nose, enormous ears and eyes, and the baby face of the Rabbit *Oryctolagus cuniculus* identify with all the attributes of human infancy. Its nature is timid, retiring and helpless, it is wholly herbivorous, and it never attacks man. Consequently this species has been cast in every likeable, cheerful role from Brer Rabbit to Bugs Bunny and Bright Eyes. But there is more than a soppy emotional response to the Rabbit. It has been a farmed food source, a provider of fur, a terribly destructive pest which rendered vast tracts of the world's land useless, and is the staple prey for several of Britain's principal predators. It has also been the victim of a spectacularly successful virus, which has routed its populations, with drastic consequences for man, downland and its inhabitants.

The Rabbit is not a British native. Although the Romans farmed it in Britain, it appears that it was only successfully introduced during the reign of the Plantagenets (AD 1159–1199). At this time the Crusades were in full swing and the increased traffic across Europe was bringing many new goods into Britain. By 1242 the first commercial Rabbit warrens, originally known as 'Coneygarths', were in operation and in the next few decades Rabbits became part of the tariff payable to the Crown by all regional land owners. Hundreds of 'conyis' or 'coneys' were supplied to Royal feasts and no doubt many escaped *en route* to establish themselves in the wild. Cries of protest were already recorded in 1254 – the Rabbit had arrived and was spreading. By 1350 we were exporting them, in 1460 there were Rabbit cookery books on the shelves, and by 1590 they had scurried into nearly every corner of the British mainland. By 1700 they had conquered Ireland too. Despite this remarkable spread, they remained scarce in many places outside the warrens, especially away from soft sandy areas where they could burrow easily to hide from predators. Then in the last half of the 19th century there was a population explosion.

The agricultural advances which led to greater food production, and the fashionable rise of game preservation for shooting, which in turn led to the mindless slaughter of avian and mammalian predators, gave the Rabbit a free rein at last. Their response was phenomenal. There were more than 30 million Rabbits burrowing by the end of the 1930s. After the Second World War, during which control had been lax, numbers had risen to a staggering 100 million, all chewing on every inch of down, scrub and wasteland. But as extraordinary as this increase had been, the population collapse that immediately followed in 1953 was catastrophic.

Fifty years earlier a mysterious disease had suddenly killed all of the experimental Rabbits housed in a hospital in Montevideo. This disease was eventually identified as a form of influenza which occurred naturally, and largely non-fatally, in the Brazilian Rabbit. The hospital's Rabbits had been European and had no immunity to the virus, known as Myxoma, and quickly succumbed. It transpired that nothing other than European Rabbits were affected, not even Hares *Lepus capensis* could contract it. Of course man, by now largely sick of the sight of the Rabbit, was quick to recognise the potential of this virus. In 1936 the Rabbit Destruction Committee of New South Wales, Australia, financed tests at Cambridge. These proved beyond doubt that this disease was the miracle cure that everyone was looking for. In Australia, where the problem was acute, Rabbits began to die in their millions following the virus's introduction. Curiously in Britain, tests with the now acclaimed myxomatosis proved ineffective and it was not until a frustrated French scientist, with a lawn full of Rabbit holes near Paris, introduced it to Europe that it really took off. Within six weeks of releasing two infected Rabbits his problem was solved. Within six months half the Rabbits in France were dead.

In the autumn of 1953 the first British cases appeared in Sussex and Kent, undoubtedly the result of artificial introductions. Farmers with infected stock freely gave contaminated Rabbits to others, who came from all over the country to collect them. With their help myxomatosis spread rapidly. Unbeknown to them the real currency of the disease in Britain was the Rabbit Flea *Spilopsyllus cuniculi*. These parasites are brilliantly designed vectors. They cling to the ears of their host and using specialist mouthparts feed on its infected blood. Only when they detect that a doe Rabbit is pregnant do they detach from the ear and descend into her nest to lay their eggs. When the larvae hatch they feed initially on the detritus at the bottom of the nest, but later successfully attach themselves to the newborn Rabbits, called kittens, thus passing on the virus to the next generation. The kittens soon become deaf and blind, their heads swell and vile pus oozes from their noses and eyes. They waddle obliviously into the open where they either rot to death or are predated.

Initially myxomatosis was 99 per cent lethal and the Rabbit became a comparative rarity. Today the virulence is reduced and immunity has risen so that the population resembles that at which it remained for the 700 years up until the population explosion. This disease will never exterminate the Rabbit, because their capacity for rapid breeding, resilience to our climate, and changing land usage mean that if local populations crash they soon recover. When they become so dense that the disease is more effectively spread, they crash again, each time with a slightly greater inbred immunity. The Rabbit as a species seems to have retained its cheerfulness through all of the horrible purges we have waged against it. They remain the largest wild herbivores affecting our downland and without their continued presence the fate of this habitat would be even more precarious.

When natural food abounds the herbivorous antics of the Rabbit resemble, supplement, or even replace those of sheep, in maintaining an open, flower-filled sward and preventing the invasion of scrub. Unfortunately, this condition is only a small hop away from the total destruction of the turf which soon follows in a densely populated Rabbit territory. It appears that the longer a piece of chalk grassland is subjected to grazing by Rabbits alone, the more the short pile of the turf lifts away from the surface of the soil. Unlike sheep, the lightweight Rabbits do not consolidate it as they graze and this condition renders the sward highly vulnerable to drought, scorching where the Rabbits urinate, to the scuffing of feet and hooves and to damage by the numerous scrapes which they dig in search of food. Rabbits tend to favour young succulent buds, shoots, leaves and flowers, but will even turn to dry and dead grass as well as roots. Nettles, burdocks, ragworts, mulleins, nightshades and stonecrops are all avoided and consequently the appearance of these shooting through the closely-grazed, fescue turf is a sure sign of a large Rabbit population. The enrichment of the mounds surrounding the warren with rabbit urine allows most of these species to grow to impressive proportions, and at the beginning of the summer these showy plants are a great attraction to insects. By the end of the year, however, the habitat takes on a desolate and neglected appearance, accentuated on the steeper slopes by serious soil erosion. Each small rabbit scrape is exaggerated by rainfall as the shallow soil is washed away to leave patches of bare chalk, looking like gleaming white scars on the hillsides.

The characteristics of continued sheep grazing are altogether different. The entire pasture is neatly trimmed to within a few centimetres of the soil and has no rank patches or bare ground, other than the strings of sheep paths which lace up and down the slopes. This uniformity is dependent on the skill of the shepherd who moves his animals around the down as the season allows. The sheep themselves actually graze by bringing the incisors of their lower jaw up against a hard toothless pad on the upper jaw and biting. Compared with cattle they distribute a relatively small quantity of dung and urine evenly over the sward and therefore the amount of scorching and fouling is minimal. Cattle on the other hand destructively wrap their tongues around the foliage, and pull rather than bite it off. This enables them to pull up even fairly well anchored plants. They produce a far greater volume of excrement and the resulting greater scorching kills much of the herbage. The ensuing enrichment of these patches of soil with nitrogen and potassium also encourages the establishment of eutrophic grasses and herbs. Those plants already present as small tussocks, tillers or rosettes, increase to enormous size. Others such as the Stinging Nettle *Urtica dioica* and Creeping Thistle *Cirsium arvense* invade the sward as seeds. The finer species soon disappear through competition with these larger, coarser plants. At the same time the soil is badly puddled and compacted. All in all, cattle are not great news for downland.

Aside from Rabbits, other wild herbivores that appear on downland include the Roe Deer *Capreolus capreolus* which can often be watched with distant caution as it emerges at dusk to browse. Because Brambles are of predominant importance in their diet, grasses are rarely grazed, this species's influence, which is only slight, is exacted on the scrub rather than the open down. That rotund muncher, the Field Vole *Microtus agrestis* is a similar case, because, although they are gluttons for ripe grass leaves and stems, they need the thick litter layer of ungrazed grassland in which to bury their tunnels and to hide from predators and are thus rarely seen on the grazed downland. Their numbers fluctuate wildly on a three to five year cycle; in a peak year thousands may be chewing their way through the scrub and such an abundance of small herbivores ideally supports several mammalian predators, the most fierce of which are the seemingly identical, long thin brown tubes of the Stoat *Mustela erminea* and the Weasel *M. nivalis*.

THE STOAT AND THE WEASEL

This pair of Mustelids have the typical elongate body shape and are highly active, solitary carnivores. They are superficially similar in terms of appearance, habits and diet, but Stoats are approximately twice the size of Weasels and this significantly effects their foraging strategies. Weasels specialise in catching rodents. They move in pulses, like battery operated toys with faulty connections. They jerk forwards, backwards and then sideways in senseless bursts of acceleration. Their bounding gait is ideal for propelling these little, light, short-legged tubes as fast as possible through the tangles of undergrowth. The narrow causeways between Bramble fronds, Hawthorn stumps and beneath confused canopies of Cow Parsley *Anthriscus sylvestris* are probed at a roller coaster pace. Here, where the light is filtered through layers of leaves, these viperine bandits explode with the same reptilian potency and slip easily onto the heels of escaping voles, shrews and mice. These are dashed in a rolling bundle of red and brown, and deleted neatly with a squeak.

Stoats on the other hand are more generalist predators and their greater size enables them to catch prey as large as Rabbits, although birds, especially ground nesters, mice and voles also feature prominently in their diet. Prey is tracked by scent and once on to a trail they are dangerously diligent. Rabbits may be relentlessly pursued through a warren whilst their comrades continue to nibble the turf. After a chase the target sometimes simply gives up, lying down squealing until the Stoat dispatches it. The death blow is always a bite to the back of the neck, and it is odd to note that if any blood is spilt the Stoat gently laps it up before beginning to eat, an observation which led to the tale that Stoats were blood suckers. Despite their violent tendencies, Stoats will also choose more meagre prey, such as insects or worms; a female was once seen delivering a number of earth worms to her young.

The difference in size between these two species and the resulting difference in diet is no doubt what allows them to share the same areas of grassland. They are not competing for the same prey, so there is room for both to forage in the same way. However, it is interesting that within both species there is a marked sexual dimorphism, males being one and a half times larger than females. It seems that a similar dividing up of the available resources is occurring between the sexes and that the smaller females feed more efficiently on smaller prey. Their reduced size also means that they have a lower total energy requirement and can therefore devote more energy to reproduction. Males are the larger of the two sexes because bigger, stronger males are probably more likely to hold larger territories containing more females with which to mate. This dimorphism is less marked in Stoats, where males feed more above ground on Rabbits and females shoot about through the vole runs underground. In Weasels, where both sexes are confined to these tunnels, competition between the sexes is intense and the size difference is exaggerated.

The problem with these theories is that they have not been fully tested by observations. Both of these animals are very difficult to observe in the field and do not behave rationally in captivity. You may catch glimpses of them bounding along a stretch of footpath, or even crossing a road, but long term behaviour is hard to watch. The best view I ever had was provided by a Weasel that was systematically exploring the mouseholes on the platform of a rural railway station. Here, relatively free of cover, I could see the sparkle in his little black eyes as he tore about, seeming incapable of any slow movements. In and out, back and forth, over and under, he left me feeling quite exhausted and certainly glad that I wasn't a dozy House Mouse from Lower Bumbleswade.

On our dingy, dismal and damp island, exotic fauna is in short supply and readily obvious. Kingfishers and Golden Orioles outshine our bevy of 'little brown jobs' in the bird stakes, whilst Meadow Browns pale into insignificance compared to Brimstones and Purple Emperor butterflies. It is sometimes sad but glamour is always a grabber. It is the Bardots, Monroes, and Brandos that evoke hero worship and legend. It is the same with our plants. I am not about to devote a passage to the sedges or fleaworts. This is about the Burnt, the Military, the Monkey and the Lizard Orchids. These beautiful and often bizarre monocotyledons are in an exotic class of their own and they have the looks and the legends to outshine any Hollywoodies. But first let me expand your vocabulary:

or+chid (',:kid) n. any terrestrial or epiphytic plant of the family Orchidaceae, having flowers of unusual shapes and beautiful colours, specialised for pollination by certain insects [from Greek orchis,
-ios or eós, a testicle, see below]

or+chido+crime (',:kido'kraim) n. an act or omission prohibited and punishable by law (Wildlife and Countryside Act 1981) and relating to plants of the Orchidaceae family, usually involves transplanting for selfish motive, annual and widespread, an evil act [from orchid (see above) and old French, from Latin crímen verdict, accusation, crime]

or+chido+phil.i.a (',:kido'filia) n. the condition of being severely, even dangerously attracted to plants of the family Orchidaceae. –
or+chido+phile (',:kido' fail) or
orchido+'phil.i.ac. n., adj.

or+chido+twitch (',:kido'twits) n, vb. 1. rapid, long-distance journey to obtain visual satisfaction from rare members of the Orchidaceae family of plants, usually undertaken by parties of poorly organised, poorly dressed males: generally uncomfortable and often disappointing. 2. Nervous disorder brought on by exposure to rare orchids,

LEFT **A dazzling** *Dactylorhiza*
RIGHT **Military Orchid**

symptoms include inane verbal diarrhoea, botanical narrow-mindedness and extreme wastage of photographic film on a single subject. 3. High frequency vibration exhibited by any rare orchid as soon as it is confronted with camera equipment, making photography impossible [from orchid (see above) and Old English twiccian to pluck; related to Old High German zwecction to pinch, Dutch twicken] – 'twitch+er (s) n.

All orchidophiles covet para-pornographic full frontal portraits of their favourite orchids. They orchidotwitch, in both the noun and verb form, and the weaker succumb to vile orchidocrimes. Cases of orchidicide are rare but increasing. Cure for these afflictions is unknown. The whole phenomenon is seasonal, with a heinous peak in late June and July. The number of virulent cases is impossible to discern. I myself have had a serious orchid habit since 1983, about the same time as I became an ice-cream addict.

Trying to put my finger on my favourite orchids is literally very difficult. I have a small notebook full of fragments of conversations held in the field, overheard in public houses, or even in the backs of friends' cars. Nothing is sacred. When I was lying beside a Bog Orchid *Hammarbya paludosa*, a man almost told me where the 'Kent Monkeys' were. Three twisted interrogations, over three years, were needed to locate the Late Spider Orchids *Ophrys fuciflora*. Perhaps the greatest goal, the Lady's Slipper Orchid *Cypripedium calceolus* was easy. A man who stood watching a beautiful, adult, male Red-footed Falcon came right out with the site, even quoting a map reference from memory. His preoccupation with the bird was a total bonus! I deduced the whereabouts of the 'Suffolk Militaries' from other unconcerned bird watchers, and was later led to their Chiltern cousins to film them (the very excuse I needed to gloat over these prizes of our plant fauna). However, Dark Red Helleborine *Epipactis atrorubens*, Ghost Orchid *Epipogium aphyllum*, Irish Lady's Tresses *Spiranthes romanzoffiana*, Fen Orchid *Liparis loeselii* and Small White

Orchid *Pseudoorchis albida* currently remain vacant memories, although I have snippets of directions relating to them all. Such intense desire is healthy. I have never intentionally damaged any plant or its habitat to satiate my cravings. Indeed, this is the antithesis of the disease. A few trespassing sessions maybe, a lot of boring conversations for my friends to endure undoubtedly, and an excess of adrenalin certainly!

Please don't think I'm sitting smugly, knowing where these things appear, whilst some of you, who would long to see them, do not. The pursuit of the sites sorts the casually curious from the seriously dedicated, and that's why I am not going to irresponsibly publish the precise whereabouts of the following gems. But I will tease and tantalise you with descriptions of five of the most dangerously attractive and highly desirable orchids.

THE MILITARY ORCHID

The Military and Monkey Orchids belong to the genus *Orchis*, which also includes the Lady *O. purpurea*, Green Winged *O. morio*, Early Purple *O. mascula*, and Burnt *O. ustulata* Orchids. Both are very rare in Britain; in fact the Military *O. militaris* was considered extinct by the late 1920s. Then, 27 years later, a thriving colony was discovered in Buckinghamshire and, although this site survives today with a small number of plants flowering every year, a site in Suffolk, discovered in 1954, is far more impressive. An Open Day is held once a year at the latter site, where visitors are allowed to walk on catwalks over a shaded chalkpit where many flowering spikes can be examined and photographed.

In the second week in May the Military Orchid's flower spike is in only embryonic form. It appears as a broad, anaemic bud: dull, puce and unwanton, composed of many budlets. When it bursts at the end of the month it is superb. I don't know how much of my wonder was enhanced by the long wait and the long journey to a secret site, or from the sheer magic of this botanical firework. Each flower is a beautifully sculptured effigy of a violet-coated brigadier, his chest emblazoned with a crust of purple hairs and warts resembling rows of buttons and braid. These dinky soldiers wear a pallid mauve helmet with an open visor which caps a short curved spur, full of nectar for bees and flies. The ranks are massed in the first few days of June, and the spikes may almost rival the enormous Lady Orchids in size. They are truly impressive, the stalks being as robust as Asparagus, and probably just as tasty!

THE MONKEY ORCHID

The Monkey Orchid *O. simia* is more wiry limbed than the Military and instantly appears more mischievous, each flower resembling a definitely playful Spider Monkey. Equipped with red-violet lobes for legs and arms, it has a central, reduced 'limb' which is definitely more phallic than tail-like. The globular and untidy flower spikes are uncanny in that the flowers open from the top of the spikes downwards, a complete reversal of the pattern in all our other orchid species. This means that the plant is at its aesthetic peak for a very short time. As soon as the monkeys that were the first to open, and are thus the first to expire, have died their swinging playmates below are crowned in a shrivelled brown mass of lobes and labellums.

Historically speaking, the history of the British Monkey Orchid is almost comically chequered. Up until the middle of the nineteenth century the orchid was common on the chalkhills that lace parts of the Thames valley, but by the 1920s there was only one good site remaining in the Chilterns. In 1933 more than thirty spikes were picked from here and a few years later the whole area was ploughed with sub-disastrous results. Some tubers were rescued and replanted with only limited success. However, seed from these may have germinated to provide the only contemporary Chiltern site on an area of rough downland

A shrivelled Chiltern Monkey

nearby. This dry skullcap yields very pale, pinky-mauve flowers, scarcely marked, held on small, stunted almost pathetic plants. Looking as if a good sprinkler system would help, these wizened primates do not rival their Kent counterparts which are often really super plants.

During the 1950s there was a flourishing colony of Monkey Orchids on the lawn of a vicarage in Kent and each year the diligent Vicar took the seed capsules and broadcast them on the hills nearby. This task was last performed in 1955, because on the retirement of the old Vicar his successor (a man not so impressed by 'All things bright and beautiful') would not undertake to safeguard the colony. Consequently all of the plants were moved with great care to some private land nearby. Here they flowered for only one year and have since never reappeared – an act of God? In 1955, a single Monkey Orchid flowered in East Kent but was eaten by a horse – an act of Horse! Fortunately some more Monkeys appeared in the following year and a Mr. Wilks, on behalf of the Kent Trust for Nature Conservation, hand pollinated these to ensure that seed was set. This back breaking and tricky task was performed every year until 1965 when there was a thriving colony of 205 flowering spikes. These now reappear annually and are much stronger, more robust and richly marked than the original Chiltern plants. They have also spread to a handful of other localities nearby. All the Kent sites are wardened but public access is permitted and they are well worth a visit, especially in late May and early June when they are at their best.

THE BURNT ORCHID

The Burnt, or Burnt-tip Orchid, *O. ustulata* is another *Orchis* species, but one which has a much wider distribution. Its main sites lie in the south and south east of England where the undisturbed chalk pasture, which is its major habitat, persists in great abundance. It also occurs in a second area, on the limestones of the Midlands and the North of England; in North Lincolnshire, Derbyshire, Westmorland and Cumberland. However, it is without doubt a plant in decline, facing many problems under modern agricultural techniques. Being so small it cannot grow where the grass is long and at one site I visit annually the flowers seem to do best on the sides of well worn paths. It also favours sheltered sunny places which are often south facing and always well drained.

For me, Burnt Orchids are not really in the totally overwhelming plant bracket. They are too small and look as if they have been lying around in someone's jacket pocket for rather too long. They look as if they have been scorched, hence the name, and all of the details have been burned away, leaving only a mutant beauty. They are crudely marked as if little girls had been trying out their mothers' make-up. Fat-faced, pretty but definitely not beautiful, they lack the complexion of their elder, the Lady Orchid, which their individual

flowers superficially resemble. Their compact cylindrical spike is at its peak before the top flowers open, because it is then that these are still rich with a browny-violet colour and the plant has its burnt-tipped appearance. When the flowers open they rapidly fade whilst emitting a strong sweet scent which attracts a variety of insects. Seed is set in a high proportion of flowers so these pollinators obviously perform a more efficient task than those that visit the Military and Monkey Orchids, where very few ripe seed-pods can be found later in the summer.

THE STINKING RANCID GOAT ORCHID

The Lizard Orchid *Himantoglossum hircinum* is simply the most bizarre 'beast' that you will ever see. Its flowering spike is a long cluster of grey and pale green springs which uncoil into a wiry alien infestation of tangled tails and frilled legs. An abuse of symmetry, steeped in a stench of sour goats.

As I write the crippled upper parts of one of these plants lies propped in a jam jar on my windowsill. This I rescued from a windswept and desolate Kent beach with some vain hope of hand pollinating, and then broadcasting seeds in suitable locations nearer my home. The site examined held 44 plants of which 22 had attempted to flower. Many, like my room mate, had become desiccated and had snapped off, and only a small proportion had survived intact to attempt pollination. This famed site is set on some old stabilised sanddunes and in the past has given rise to as many as 200 flowering spikes in one season. This year it looked bad; all had centre partings, the flowers having all been blown to one side of the spike, many were sick or dead and, in the rain and wind, these looked like stragglers being blown back into the English Channel.

Elsewhere in Britain, Lizard Orchids flower regularly at one small Cambridgeshire site and elsewhere sporadically on their favoured calcareous soils. Their individual flowers are quite extraordinary.

Lizard Orchid

Basically grey-green, sometimes with a pinkish tinge, the five sepals and petals are rounded into a neat, closed helmet, the inside of which is marked with a series of red and brown dots and dashes which just show through to the outer surface. The three-lobed lip is remarkable; its lateral lobes are long, waxy brown structures which are neatly crinkled and recurved under the central lobe. The central lobe may be five or six centimetres long, again a waxy brown, fitted with a cleft at its point and with a white base which is marked with bright crimson hairy dots. This of course resembles the tail of the lizard and the crinkly lobes its legs. Quite where its forelimbs and head have gone is beyond me; perhaps it should be renamed the Rat Orchid, or the Kite Orchid, or the Stinking Rancid Goat Orchid. I suppose none match the reptilian ring of the current name.

Historically speaking, Lizard Orchids have enjoyed mixed fortune in Britain. First noted in 1641, in Kent, it continued to wriggle here until 1805 when it completely disappeared and became a plant of extreme rarity, restricted to a handful of sporadic sites in south east England. Then, in a remarkable change of fortune, there was a veritable explosion of Lizard Orchids and they appeared as far north as Yorkshire and west as Devon. This outburst peaked in the 1930s and was probably in response to a change to a more oceanic climate, resembling that of north west France where they are said to 'flourish in abundance'. Since this time there has been another decline and today the 'Lizzies' are aggregated into Kent, Sussex and Cambridgeshire, although other counties seem to have the odd, legendary plant dotted along their chalky slopes, car parks and roadsides. If you ever get the goaty whiff of one of these devils, see it. With the exception of the infamous Ghost Orchid they are the greatest botanical spectacle in Britain and will undoubtedly burst your brain. They did mine!

AN ORCHID WITHOUT A POLLINATOR

Going back to my roots, there is the Bee Orchid *Ophrys apifera*, the first orchid of the *Ophrys* group that I saw. This marvellous group includes the Fly Orchid, and both the Early and Late Spider Orchids, two rarities of the South Coast. All of these species are flowers which mimic the bodies of certain Hymenopteran insects with which the earlier emerging male insects attempt to copulate. During this futile attempt, the orchid's pollenia sticks to the frustrated insect, and is soon transferred to another look-alike mate. A marvel of evolution, that the British Bee Orchids cannot use. It appears that the pollinator it has evolved to attract, a solitary bee *Eucera* sp., only occurs in the Mediterranean area. In this country it is, therefore, only successful self-pollination which allows the species to persist. It is a marvellous flower and appears commonly every year as far north as southern Scotland, making it readily available to any budding orchidophile. But be careful, it could be the start of a terrible disease!

AN ORCHID EXPERT

One of the most chronically affected orchidophiles I have ever met is a good friend of mine, Gerry Mundey. Born and bred in Henley-on-Thames he was well placed to explore the Chilterns and fondly recounts innumerable trips to see Military, Monkey and the elusive Ghost Orchids. Whilst wardening these in the early seventies Gerry decided he could be better employed. Undaunted by the legends and unconcerned by the impossible enigmas, perpetrated by Victorian ignorance persisting to this day, Gerry set out to grow our orchids from seed. For an ex-Shell executive and underwater cameraman this meant starting from scratch.

Gerry moved to Hampshire and secured the night time loan of a special laboratory at a local veterinary company. Simultaneously, he began corresponding with the Canberra Botanic Gardens in Australia where some native species were just beginning to thrive in culture. Making the necessary modifications, and rapidly perfecting his own sterile techniques, he soon developed a reputation as one of the world's terrestrial orchid culture pioneers. As Gerry points out, the more obscure the subject you choose, the quicker and easier it is to become the alleged authority. In this unenviable position, surrounded by over a thousand sterile bottles sprouting orchid seeds in a lonely laboratory, Gerry got into rather a tight spot.

Somewhere in southern Africa a long lost orchid, last seen in 1840, was re-discovered in the baking bush. There was only one, and it was picked. Fortunately, this was only half of a tragedy because some seed was gleaned from the damaged specimen. Knowing of his famed techniques, the biologists sent this to Gerry, no doubt a little desperate for success. When the seed arrived it had been rather foolishly wrapped in silver foil, had sweated during transport, got damp, and become infected by a gargantuan blob of rampant fungus. Also enclosed was a letter outlining that a special reserve had been set up to hold the plants that Gerry would culture. Gazing at the material he must have felt under a little pressure!

Initial attempts to germinate the seeds produced an accelerated growth of fungus, which sprouted forth after a few days, resulting in the destruction of the seeds and the sterile technique. At this point, it is worth outlining that orchid seeds are microscopic, have negligible weight, and are prone to blow away in any slight draught, which is how they are usually dispersed. Gerry describes them as looking like tiny tennis balls pushed into socks made of a string vest. They are composed of between 20 and 120 undifferentiated cells, the larger of which become the shoot and the smaller the roots. There are no food reserves which is why a fungus is needed to aid the plant through germination, up until the time when chlorophyll can be produced to photosynthesise and provide the plant with energy for future growth. Because of this malnourished start, immense numbers of seeds are produced by each plant, many British species giving rise to at least 6,000 and some of the tropical orchids to over a million per pod. In any case, the hundreds or thousands that formed the soggy little pile of rare South African orchid were totally useless.

With a degree of reasoning, which he assures me was calm and calculating, Gerry's eyes began to wander around his laboratory. They strayed onto one of life's most powerful toxins, Industrial Methylated Spirit. In what I would call a 'desperate' rather than a 'calm' attempt, Gerry soaked the remaining seeds in a dish full of meths for one and a half hours. He then transferred them to a dish full of powerful household bleach for three and a half hours. He recounts that the half hours were added because he got carried away with his newspaper! Amazingly enough, when strained, dried and sown in new sterile jars, the seeds germinated and produced adult plants, the descendants of which now grow on some parched fragment of an African nature reserve.

Since this heroic, face-saving feat, Gerry has concentrated on germinating British terrestrial orchids with more or less similar success. He finds that the growth to first flowering is extended by a year compared to those plants growing in the wild. This is because of the inefficiency of nutrient intake by his cultured plants, when provided with only a solution of chemicals. When gripped by a 'fungus helper', under natural conditions, the input of nutrients is super-efficient and leads to earlier flowering. The 'fifteen year to first flowering' legends which surround orchids such as the Burnt-tip, are nonsense and arose from ancient examination of their protocorms (bulbs). By counting rings on parts of these structures and on presuming that these were annual growth rings, botanists decided that these species took an inordinately long time before first flowering. In fact they can probably flower after only three years. The *Dactylorhiza* genera of Spotted and Marsh Orchids, the Green-winged, Fragrant and most other leafy, green terrestrial species soon become independent from any fungal partner, required for germination. Most of these can be grown in culture by replacing the fungus with a nutrient medium full of sugar as an energy source. Indeed this technique has currently enabled the laboratory at Kew Gardens in London to culture seeds from the sole remaining Lady's Slipper Orchid growing in Yorkshire.

For other species, the precise fungus required is grown on an otherwise sterile medium to which the seeds are added. This gives far better and quicker results, mimicking the natural process. However, the fungus must be starved into submission. Fed too well, it becomes rampant and consumes rather than aids the tender orchid plantlet. Using this technique, Military, Monkey, Lady and Burnt Orchids could soon be furiously blossoming in specialists' greenhouses. The one current stumbling block is the *Epipactis* group of Helleborines. Despite an inordinate amount of effort, these remain impossible to germinate and raise to the flowering stage under cultured conditions. The exact fungi have not been isolated and the fact that the fungal-plant relationship persists throughout the life of the plant undoubtedly makes this task more difficult.

Far from being an expensive, exclusive and time consuming hobby for a few devoted scientists the ability to germinate and grow our British orchids should be an important conservation technique. The Military, Monkey, Lizard, Late Spider, Early Spider, Lady and Lady's Slipper Orchids are each restricted to a handful of sites in the British Isles. In the last forty years an area the size of Berkshire, Bedfordshire, Buckinghamshire and Oxfordshire has disappeared under concrete. Ninety-five per cent of our flower-rich meadows have gone under the plough, and the decline of our chalk grasslands through agricultural change and scrub encroachment has been rife. Consequently, our orchids have suffered a devastating habitat loss, and 'orchidocrime', far from being a trite play on words, is a real phenomenon that sees devoted groups of volunteers guarding our remaining colonies of rare species each summer season. Just as with egg collecting it is British collectors who are digging up the rare British orchids, not for money, but to satisfy their own cravings. These activities are obviously illegal yet few orchidocriminals are ever brought before the Courts to suffer charges and punishment imposed by our Wildlife and Countryside Act. The problem is not entirely British; the Japanese, the Taiwanese, and worst of all the Chinese are currently digging and selling every species of their orchid floras by the thousand. To import one of the rarest Chinese orchids you need only apply for a permit, which, without fail, comes by return of post, and then, at your own cost, you can further endanger one of the world's most precariously balanced plants. This situation will not be rectified whilst we, the British, make little attempt to stop this destructive trade.

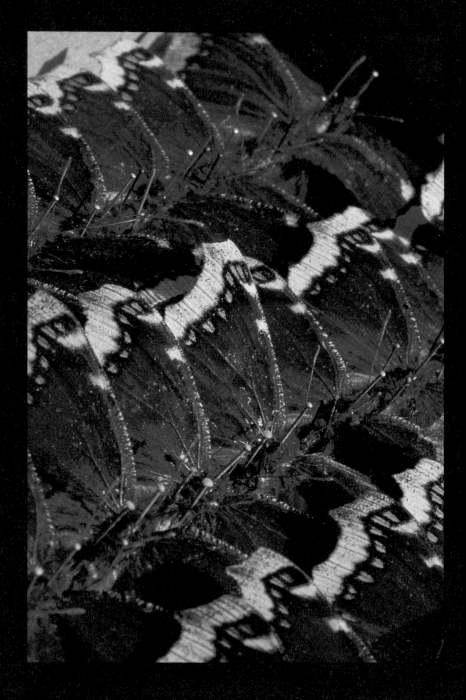

It is pitch black and parched. It smells of dust, of old furniture, of age itself. There is no movement at all, not even a breath of air. There is not a sound: not the rustle of grass, the chirp of a bird, the yap of a fox, not even the hum of electricity. Time passes forever in this vacuum, a capsule which holds a sickening relict of our past. Here, bled dry, pressed, aligned in a pathetically unnatural pose and speared on a slither of sharp steel is a perfect indicator of man's insanity. Here is the hollow, dead carcass of an insect, one of the last Large Blue butterflies, and its sordid surroundings could not be more different than the bright, and open downland where it once dared to flex its steely blue wings.

Butterfly collectors will be quick to assert that they were not responsible for this species's extinction, that it had been declining for years for all sorts of reasons. Habitat loss, climate, pesticides may have all had an effect but when a species is pushed to the brink – collectors have a nasty tendency to nudge it over!

THE COLLECTORS

There is little doubt, despite many attempts to disclaim the crime, that Victorian collectors were largely responsible for the continued systematic persecution of perhaps our brightest butterfly, the Large Copper *Lycaena dispar dispar*. This striking metallic insect had its fenland habitats drained, but many of its former haunts remain to this day in their original condition, including Holme Fen, where in 1847, or 1848, some madman killed the last one. There is a concise account of butterfly collecting in E. B. Ford's *Butterflies*, a New Naturalist first published in 1945. The first chapter details the exploits of entomologists from their earliest days up until the Victorian era when this habit ran riot. Ford, himself a collector, counts it as a privilege to have known some fellow enthusiasts from the 1850s and 60s whom he recalls as being

LEFT **A dead regiment of rarity**
RIGHT **Marbled White**

'fine naturalists'. Their knowledge, he says, was largely empirical and died with them, and he rarely found their like in his day. There is it seems, even amongst contemporary naturalists and conservationists, a feeling that butterfly collecting does little harm to the remnants of our battered populations, an excuse no doubt formerly voiced on that other diabolical and fortunately now outlawed habit of egg collecting. However, in these days of intensive farming, agricultural development and wholesale habitat destruction, the pressures on these insects are not what they were even forty years ago, and the collection of any gravid female butterfly is going to substantially reduce any small colony of that species. It is, I feel, high time that the collection of entomological specimens be entirely confined to those engaged in proper scientific research, and that this antiquated and selfish habit be relegated to the same class as egg collecting. Those who persist in it should face similar fines and definite alienation in this, what purports to be, the age of concern for conservation and ecological enlightenment.

Today, somewhere in Britain is a person who occasionally pulls open a drawer to gloat over the last Large Copper. I hope he never gets a wink of sleep, but precisely what did happen more recently to the Large Blue *Maculinea arion*?

THE LARGE BLUE

Numerous attempts were made to save this beautiful insect, but all were unsuccessful. It had been declining for at least a hundred years, and by the 1950s it was only known from thirty or forty sites. Only four of these sites still had Large Blues ten years later. In 1969, 1970 and 1973, respectively, Large Blues disappeared from three of these sites, leaving only one to struggle to the end of the seventies. By 1972, however, it was clear that the ecology of the species had never been fully understood, and a research programme was initiated by Jeremy Thomas of the Nature Conservancy Council in an attempt to save the species. Over five years the factors affecting annual fluctuations in numbers were concisely studied and surveys were made of the former habitats, distribution, status, local races, lifecycles and behaviour of the butterfly. Finally, the sad task of analysing the habitat of the last existing site was undertaken. All of this research revealed that the Large Blue had an incredibly specialised lifecycle dependent on two important factors.

The first was the presence of Thyme *Thymus praecox*, on to the buds of which the butterfly lays its eggs. Here, for the first period of the larval stage, the young caterpillars munch through the flower. Later, however, they are carried off by one, and one only, species of Red Ant *Myrmica sabuleti* – the second factor – which are attracted to the caterpillar by sugary secretions from a gland on the caterpillar's back. The ants take the caterpillars to their nest, where the caterpillar spends nine months feeding on the ants' grubs before pupating to later emerge as an adult. The caterpillars only thrived in this single species of ants' nest, and the ants only survive where the turf is kept short by regular grazing.

For much of this century downland has become unprofitable for farming and the hill-sides frequented by the ants, and in turn Large Blues, were abandoned. In the 1950s, when these butterflies began their final, steep and slippery slide to extinction, myxomatosis decimated the Rabbit population and the deterioration of any remaining habitat rapidly followed. The hill-sides that were once clad in Thyme were now rank grassland going on Hawthorn scrub and frequented by commoner butterflies such as Chalkhill Blues *Lysandra coridon*, Common Blues *Polyommatus icarus* and Marbled Whites *Melanargia galathea*.

By 1973 the Large Blue persisted as one fragile and delicate population, but by this stage Jeremy Thomas was able to develop a management plan that would best suit the butterfly. Heavy grazing of the site produced a sward only one centimetre high, in turn encouraging the necessary numbers of *M. sabuleti*. Any lighter grazing led to an increase in a similar species of ant, but larvae abducted by workers of this species suffered a five times higher mortality than those tended by *M. sabuleti*. With the help of an army of sheep the grazing was controlled, and the population of butterflies began to rise. However, it was clear that the carrying capacity of this site was low and that even the largest population that it could support would be unable to withstand any occasional adverse conditions. Overcrowding began to occur when larvae entered the ants' nests. In one case about forty were taken underground and all died from starvation as the limited number of grubs available in one nest was not sufficient to support that number of caterpillars. As a result of this the population declined from 300 adults in 1973 to only 100 in 1974, purely due to a low density of the necessary ants.

Following this, the severe droughts of 1975 and 1976 had a catastrophic effect, and the population crashed to 16 adults in 1977. By this time the site had definitely been improved for the butterfly, but the population was so low that it became subject to any chance factors. For example only 5 of the 16 butterflies in 1977 were females, and at least 2 failed to mate because the males, which emerge earlier and are fairly short lived, had already died. In comparison with the normal fertilisation percentage of 85 per cent of females, 40 per cent (and 40 per cent representing only 2 individuals) was a bit of a disaster. Survival of the resulting larvae was also lower than usual, so in 1978 it was decided to rear the butterflies in captivity. Only two females emerged, of which only one was mated, but from this one mating 59 larvae were hatched, reared and then fostered into ants' nests on the site, a figure much higher than would have naturally been achieved if even both pairs had successfully bred. Because of this success it was predicted that adult numbers in 1979 would be greater. Unfortunately and

inexplicably, although 22 adults emerged and were taken into captivity they all failed to pair and the population became extinct. Having acquired the knowledge he needed, Jeremy Thomas had fought a desperate battle to maintain a population that was too small to support itself, and as he glumly says, if the measures that were taken had been taken only four years earlier, the British Large Blue butterfly could still be flitting over areas of our downland today.

There was a lull after the storm and no doubt the summer of 1980 was a wretched time for Jeremy. A great treasure had slipped away after a run of random misfortunes. But by 1983 he had hatched a scheme to reintroduce the butterfly. At this stage none of the sites that remained met the criteria which he now fully understood, and it was not until 1985 that one hill-side seemed suitable, having a high density of ants' nests and Thyme plants. Thyme takes ages to colonise a suitable new habitat, so thousands of plants were introduced from specimens grown in nurseries. These were planted in the necessary ants' territories and this enabled the butterfly to be dispersed more efficiently over a much larger area.

Next, trials began to find a suitable race of European Large Blues, to introduce to the prepared site in Britain. Butterflies from the south of France proved unsuccessful, but those from Sweden gave promising results. When, in September 1983, caterpillars of this species were placed near ants' nests they were all taken underground and survived as well as our native Large Blues had done. More importantly the adults that emerged the following summer did so at the same time as the former British ones had, thus enabling the females to lay their eggs on the tight young Thyme flower buds which are essential for healthy development of the larvae. The Swedish authorities were glad to donate a few of their butterflies, and in fact these Large Blues appear very similar to the old British race. They may be slightly larger and brighter blue and even more heavily spotted, but these differences are variable and small, and only apparent to those who have been fortunate enough to examine a great many specimens.

At this stage the decision was made to make a full scale attempt at re-introduction. But, by a quirk of long deserved good fortune, when the attempt to re-trap all the emerging adults the following summer failed, several escaped, successfully bred and laid eggs over the new site. The project was proving successful even before it had the go-ahead, an unusual aspect for any conservation programme. In 1985 Jeremy enjoyed the thrill of seeing a freshly emerged female alight on a Thyme plant and begin to lay eggs. Later at least 10 butterflies appeared and by the time this trial colony had completed three generations it had already begun to increase in numbers. It had, however, been generated from just one or two females and, due to this rather limited number of founders and thus limited variation, was genetically highly unstable. To overcome this problem, new stock was flown in from Sweden. The resulting caterpillars were gently transferred to the ants' nests on the site and the genetics of the population given a successful boost. In 1987, when the most recent census was made, nearly 100 adults emerged to lay well over 2,000 eggs and 84 per cent of the larvae were adopted by the ants, compared with only 57 per cent in the best year for our old British species. If the habitat remains constant, which it should as it is carefully managed, the population will be able to increase until it reaches 800 to 850 adults. Currently this site has no public access, because of the threat of fire and disruption of grazing, but fortunately all those concerned with the re-introduction project are determined that re-establishment should occur at more sites, not only to stabilise the population, but also to allow the interested public the opportunity of enjoying these exceptional butterflies and watching their extraordinary life-cycle at first hand. This should be possible by the early 1990s and I for one cannot wait to admire this triumph of practical conservation.

OTHER ASSORTED COLOURS

The great variety of plants and the often warm slopes of the downlands of southern Britain provide a suitable habitat for a large proportion of the remaining British butterfly species. From June to August on sunny afternoons the slopes and scarps can be a twinkling carnival of soft pastel blues, whites, browns and oranges, all flickering from flower to flower probing with a flexed proboscis or homing on a pheromone with an urge to mate. Nearly always preoccupied with some such task, many of these butterflies are easily approached with practice. Little S.A.S. training is required (stun grenades are not optional). Just creep in slowly, avoiding sudden movements, casting shadows over, or disturbing vegetation in contact with the butterfly. But, whilst some species can be stalked close enough to smell, others seem frustratingly impossible to examine. For these some good close focusing binoculars are in order and in fact I have even seen some Lepidopterists behaving more like 'birders', peering deep into the foliage through powerful telescopes!

Of all the species found on downland, only three are in fact limited by any geological considerations to the chalk downs of southern England. These are the Silver-spotted Skipper *Hesperia comma*, whose rapid flight can be seen in August; the Chalkhill Blue, a furiously fast fluttering insect found from late July onwards; and the Adonis Blue *Lysandra bellargus*, which in the absence of its late, great Large Blue cousin is the most splendid of our Blue butterflies. The Chalkhill and Adonis Blue are also dependent on the distribution of their larval food plant, the Horseshoe Vetch *Hippocrepis comosa*. Both of their green and yellow striped, woodlouse look-alike larvae feed on this plant and may also depend on an abundance of certain ant species to guard their well-being. The Little

Black-veined White

Blue *Cupido minimus* frequently occurs on downs and rough grassy slopes but has a wide distribution across southern England, thriving in well defined colonies which may re-emerge year after year. The Brown Argus *Aricia agestis* shows an inclination toward chalk and limestone hills where its food plant the Common Rockrose *Helianthemum nummularium* grows, but it also has an alternative food source, the Storksbill *Erodium cicutarium*, more typically a plant of sandy soils. This species can thus be found as far north as the Western Isles, flying over sand-hills by the sea.

The Grayling *Hipparchia semele* is a species characteristic of dry heaths, mainly because it cannot survive in damp situations. Consequently the often parched habitat of chalkland also attracts this grass feeding species. Joining it in August, the magnificent Dark Green Fritillary *Mesoacidalia aglaja* can be seen beating effortlessly up and down short grass hill-sides whilst in stiller areas with thicker,

more rampant vegetation the pretty Marbled White and ubiquitous Meadow Brown *Maniola jurtina* search for nectar. The Ringlet *Aphantopus hyperantus* too is fond of areas of long grass, often straying to woodland rides, as are the skippers, including the Dingy *Erynnis tages*, Grizzled *Pyrgus malvae*, Large *Ochlodes venatus* and Small *Thymelicus flavus* which are all frequently encountered on a summer downland foray. The different species of skipper may initially be difficult to identify. They are often jittery and tricky to approach, and some species are only slightly different from one another, requiring exact examination to separate them. They are all small butterflies whose characteristic rapid darting flight gives them their name. At rest they appear more like moths, having relatively large bodies, heads and antennae and acting like robust, rich orange-chestnut rogues, rising rapidly from low vegetation to bully any other passing insect. If anything, the skippers are an irritating mix of butterfly and moth, although their caterpillars are unusual because they live in tubes of grass rolled together and stick fast with spider-like silk. Here they live until they wrap themselves in a loosely spun cocoon to prepare for adulthood.

I remember as a child popping a pupa in my fingers. I was disgusted at the mass of puce-green pus which oozed from this apparently inert capsule. It appeared completely amorphous, a useless rotted soup, which was beyond any miracle of metamorphosis. In fact, it was an organised emulsion of differentiated tissues engulfed in the tortuous change from larva to adult. The larval organs are destroyed completely by the insect's own blood and by the lack of a particular hormone, Juvenile Hormone, that has maintained its youth. This chemical is no longer released from the brain to infuse through its tissues and in its absence, amid the mayhem, the all important Imaginal buds begin to burst.

These buds are tiny packets of cells, which have been almost dormant through-out larval life, each the building block precursor for a set of advanced adult organs. Remarkably, even caterpillars have wings, or at least the rudiments of them hidden in the second and third segments of the body, and just before pupation these consist of tiny flaps of undifferentiated cells, lying in a pocket of skin covered by the outer cuticle. During the early stages of the pupation process the walls of the wing membranes are thick and packed with special cells to secrete the scales which give butterflies their characteristic colourful appearances. Some of these colours are produced by interference, like those seen in soap bubbles or a film of oil on a wet road. Then the shades and tones change depending upon the angle of view. But more often these scales contain red, yellow, blue or white pigments. These colours originate inside the body and are carried to the initially transparent scales in the butterflies' blood. Some scales grow more quickly than others and when the various pigments flood into the wings they

Orange-tip

downwards. At this stage its wings look like a pair of soaked and badly creased Hawaiian shirts crammed on to its shoulders. They are soft, flabby and only about a tenth of their final size, appearing 'bag-like' because the two membranes from which they are constructed remain separate until blood is forced into them. This draws them together, flattening them into thin sheets strengthened by hollow tubes. After a while they stretch to full size, but are still damp and have to be held apart until dry. Finally, when they are hard, they are literally snapped together and the adult butterfly ejects a large drop of reddish fluid from its anus. This is all the stored up excretory products of the pupal stage, because throughout its imprisonment the insect was unable to eat, drink or excrete any material. Between twenty minutes and two hours after the first pupal split the butterfly is ready to take its wings for their first flight, no doubt in search of a nectar-filled flower to quench its thirst. Just as I remember squashing my pupa, I also remember lying flat on some local wasteland watching a do so at different times. Each can only fill the tiny scale sacs at a particular stage of their development so for instance the dark blackish or brown scales develop more slowly than paler reds, yellows, or whites. Thus the colouring-in of a butterfly's wing is rather like the filling of a glass phial with coloured sand, only it is altogether far more beautiful and spectacular.

Most British butterflies pupate for about three weeks. A day or so before they emerge the wing colours are clearly visible through the pupal cases. In fact they can even be seen as a perfect miniature, in terms of colour or pattern, of the adults' wings. At the end of this stage of the life-cycle the skin of the pupa splits like a ripe fruit behind the head of the emerging insect. This then struggles forth, drawing its damp antennae, legs, and wings, carefully out of its chitinous packing case. Quite ungracefully the butterfly shuffles to a position close at hand, where it can hang tiny, slimy bogey transform into a crisp,

bright and alive Small Copper *Lycaena phlaeas*. It seemed to take an age, but the resulting article has remained one of my favourites, locked in the tangled memories of my own larval stages. The Small Copper's upper-side is marked with a brilliant metallic coppery red and its under-sides have delicate patterns on a light biscuit background. You can find this neat little chap over almost the whole of Britain but you would have to travel to isolated areas of southern England to catch a glimpse our remaining pair of downland specialities.

The Glanville Fritillary *Melitaea cinxia* is restricted to the southern coast of the Isle of Wight where it skims over a series of small seaside cliffs. In some places these steep banks may be fifteen to twenty feet in height, separated by rough grassy slopes where its essential food-plants, the Narrow Leaved and Sea Plantains *Plantago* spp. are able to root. First discovered in 1824, its range has contracted ever since then, but it still remains as a thriving and viable colony. In Europe, neither this species, nor the Lulworth Skipper *Thymelicus acteon* which is similarly restricted to an area of seaside grassland on the Isle of Purbeck, are maritime species. It appears that both species have specific temperature requirements, needing a greater amount of sunlight than our climate usually affords. In these two locations they seem to have adapted themselves to a peculiar environment that allows them to thrive. They may even have evolved physiological modifications to live here, but it is interesting that Lulworth Skippers and Glanville Fritillaries from Britain are completely indistinguishable from those found on the continent. Other butterflies, such as the Swallowtail *Papilio machaon* which has adapted to be a purely Fenland insect in England, have already taken on a different appearance than other members of the species from elsewhere in Europe. It seems that the former two species are able to survive because their numbers are not prone to violent fluctuations which run the risk of extinction on this, the edge of their ranges.

Whilst the slopes remain relatively rich in terms of butterfly fauna there is only one bird, the Skylark *Alauda arvensis*, which is at all common over our downlands today. In some areas Meadow Pipits *Anthus pratensis* nearly rival them in abundance, but generally it is only the trilling of the lark which drifts over this spartan landscape. In the past, Stone Curlews *Burhinus oedicnemus*, Wheatears *Oenanthe oenanthe* and, wherever songposts were available, Woodlarks *Lullula arborea* shared the short cropped turf, but since the demise of downland these species have decreased and are now found more often on heathlands.

Localised populations and odd pairs of Lapwings *Vanellus vanellus* can often be found on areas of downland where the gradient is not too steep, but in areas where scrub encroachment has occurred the number of birds rises dramatically. There is some difficulty in classifying the actual species typical of this habitat because it varies so dramatically in terms of its floral composition, openness and height; all predominant factors influencing the type of bird fauna that is present.

In the succession from open downland to closed canopy scrub, Linnets *Carduelis cannabina* and the Yellowhammers *Emberiza citrinella* are pioneer species, but these soon phase out as the scrub thickens. It is only Willow Warblers *Phylloscopus trochilus* and Dunnocks *Prunella modularis* that seem to persist right through from the light open canopy of scattered shrubs to the dense impenetrable forest of prickly Hawthorns, Buckthorns and Elders. By the time the habitat has reached this stage Chaffinches *Fringilla colebs*, Bullfinches *Pyrrhula pyrrhula*, Blackcaps *Sylvia atricapilla*, Song Thrushes *Turdus philomelos*, Robins *Erithacus rubecula*, Blackbirds *Turdus merula*, Wrens *Troglodytes troglodytes*, Whitethroats *Sylvia communis* and up to

LEFT **Full song**
RIGHT **Storm**

nine other species may be residents. Consequently the normally unwelcome presence of scrubland actually increases the breeding diversity and density of birds, yet many of these are typically woodland species and not real downland specialities. Just such a case is one of the most celebrated of all our birds.

THE NIGHTINGALE

Putting the notes of a bird song into words is almost impossible. There is no readily known spectrum to quote from, as there is with colour. No choice adjectives such as hard, soft, rough, or smooth, to describe its texture. Whilst nearly everyone could more or less visualise the sombre, if not unremarkable, pale chestnut brown upper-parts and rufous fawn underside of our most famous songster, to print a stave splattered with crochets, quavers and other musical dots would do little for the general reader. Besides, the song of the Nightingale *Luscinia megarhyncha* is quite beyond reproduction on a pianoforte.

At best described as a versatile mixture of throaty chuckles and rich deep phrases held with pure treble, it spans a rich quality of tonal range and is filled with trills and flourishes. Long high plaintive notes, and hard metallic chips, mean that the song of the Nightingale undoubtedly has to be heard to be understood. In the dying light, with a party of midges for company, stand in a warm pocket of a thicket staring into the hidden heart of a Hawthorn and listen to this remarkable solo. The quick clean jumps of pitch will make you twitch. The fast slurred fugue will make you think that there is a partner in this song; and the far carrying whistles lure you back every time you think that the concert has ended.

This song can be heard in the heat of the mid-day sun and in the dead of night, but it is most frequently delivered at dusk and dawn. Frustratingly, in Britain, Nightingales tend to sing from incredibly dense cover whilst, in Spain for instance, I have seen them singing openly on the edges of bushes and from sheltered fence wires. To catch the performance you must visit areas of deciduous woodland or thorn scrub from mid-April to mid-June, although the virtuosos reach their crescendo during the middle of May. For those of you in the north of Britain this will mean a trip south, because when the Nightingale returns from its West Africa wintering areas it seldom strays further north than a line from Yorkshire across to South Wales and Devon. Further, their population has recently declined, so that their highest densities now occur in south east England. Hazel coppice is the most suitable habitat for Nightingales in Britain, but with the demise of this type of woodland management the dense shrub layer, packed with brambles, wild roses, nettles and umbellifers found growing in many scrubby situations more readily holds these small thrushes. This thick ground zone of vegetation is required to provide their food, which comprises worms, beetles, caterpillars, the pupae of ants and flies, and spiders. In autumn, Nightingales will also feed on many types of berry, while stocking up reserves for their migration. Their foraging behaviour is very 'Robinesque'. They hop erratically through the scrub, constantly cocking their heads to one side and staring through big brown eyes into their poorly lit habitat. They are, of course, much more secretive than Robins.

Their ritualised pairing display is rarely seen through the dense cover. It apparently involves posturing, with drooping, flinching and fluttering wings and fanning the rich brown tail. Following this sexual skullduggery a large bulky nest is tucked away in a shaded patch of ivy or nettles, usually on, or close to, the ground. It is made from a mass of dead leaves, hairs and grasses and holds four or five olive green or brown eggs in a deep cup.

However, to see any of these things or indeed just to glimpse the flurry of a Nightingale whirring through the shade, or to hear a few fleeting notes delivered from semi-concealment, will require a great deal of patience. Then, if you are lucky, a male may select a backlit perch and, through the pallid light, allow you a brief peek at his performance. Whatever you do, don't applaud from the most exclusive seat money can't buy.

PARTRIDGES

The lowly plumage of the Nightingale is undoubtedly saved by the extraordinary appeal of its voice. The Grey Partridge *Perdix perdix* shares no such fortune. Hunchbacked and huddled, they waddle about furiously as if embarrassed by their brownness. Small parties, known as 'coveys', toil amongst the grasses in the field like ragged mediaeval serfs depressed by famine. Here they use their bills to pick through the soil for grass and weed seeds, although green leaves, cereals and clovers also combine with insects to fill their crops. In addition to the adults' requirements, sawfly and moth larvae, aphids, weevils and ground beetles are essential for the healthy growth of the Partridge chicks: without this insect component to supplement their salads the young show retarded growth and feathering, and as a result, increased mortality. With the mono-mindedness of modern agricultural techniques these 'harmful' insect pests have been 'pesticided' into near extinction, and as a result the Grey Partridge has declined drastically since the 1950s.

The reasons for this reduction are complex. Other changes in agricultural practice, such as stubble burning and autumn ploughing are also to blame. The latter causes a decrease in the population of sawfly larvae of the family Tenthredinidae, which is one of the staple foods for the young. But the problem is also biological, in that Grey Partridges have no innate ability to adjust their nesting time in response to poor weather. In this recent run of cold, wet springs there has been a shortage of food, particularly arthropods, for the newly-hatched young and this has further accelerated the decline. The passing of the Grey Partridge began on the western side of the British Isles. In Ireland the situation

was critical by the 1930s when a ban on shooting was introduced. Without this, and restocking, the species would probably be extinct in Ireland by now. Western Scotland, parts of Wales and the West Country retain only a few Partridges and only in areas where there is plenty of shrub, grass or hedgerow cover in early spring are there now high densities of this bird.

Grey Partridges are highly gregarious and roam in coveys between July and February. These are usually between 5 and 25 strong, although even larger coveys may develop temporarily if the breeding season has been successful. These groups wander within set home ranges and use a form of moving territory to achieve their spacing from other parties. Thus separate groups may forage over the same area, but strictly at different times. The degree of tolerance exhibited by any covey depends on the food availability and height of cover amongst which they are foraging.

When two groups do eventually coincide, the resulting mêlée can be almost comical; despite the obvious eruption of adrenalin in the infuriated birds. Up to 50 of these urchins may be seen chasing each other indiscriminately over a small area, jumping, fluttering their wings and careering across the soil in a sudden turmoil of aggressive activity. There seems to be no order and direction of attack or retreat as the birds wend and weave from flock to flock like crazed ants over an agitated nest. The combatants pursue one another with their necks outstretched and wings lightly extended along the sides of their body. Chases sometimes culminate in pairs of Partridges rushing head on to one another, stopping just before the inevitable collision and rearing up with breasts and bills almost touching. A harsh metallic shouting match often follows and eventually some vicious sparring follows, with birds fighting with their feet, wings and bills, aiming their blows at the top of their opponent's head. The defeated bird turns and is chased away in a half run, half flight, victory race. More often than not these chases are ritualised. Roles may be instantaneously reversed and the partridge victor may find himself turning tail and retreating back across the field of battle.

Perhaps it is a little unfair to paint the Grey Partridge as such a dowdy bird, but they are most easily seen during the winter months when the bleak white skies and bleached landscapes turn them into silhouettes and make them look like clods of loose soil. In good summer sunshine, however, they are in fact quite well marked. The male's forehead, face and throat is a rich orange buff and his grey flanks and breast are neatly marked with chestnut blotches. There is a broad dark brown inverted horseshoe mark on his belly. However, Britain's other Partridge is much more brightly coloured and altogether more conspicuous.

The Red-legged Partridge *Alectoris rufa* is not a native species and its population here has derived predominantly from stock released in Suffolk in 1790. This introduction was facilitated by the importation of several thousand eggs from France and since then over 60 further successful introductions have been made. Its distribution in Britain shows a pronounced easterly bias because East Anglia probably provides the optimal conditions of intensive agriculture and continental type of climate that it requires. Here the soils are sandy, or chalky, and dry, the rainfall is the lowest in Britain, and survival rate of the chicks is high. Some of the more conservative of the shooting fraternity believe that the Red-legged Partridge only affords poor sport, compared to the native Grey, and with this in mind attempts have been made to eliminate it from a few areas. However by the 1970s Red-legs had spread their range more than ever and could be found on sandy heaths, chalk downlands, coastal shingle and dunes and in woodland wherever large glades or wide rides provided them with foraging habitat.

The Red-legged Partridge shares many of the same behavioural traits as its cousin the Grey. It too is gregarious in winter when coveys of up to 70, or exceptionally 200 to 300, may congregate. These are less aggressive than the Grey Partridge and may mix, if they meet, with little or no antagonism. At dusk, the coveys become restless and as an anti-predator strategy, to prevent any tracking by scent of the birds, they suddenly take to the wing and return to one faithful roosting site, either on the ground or in trees. Before dawn the birds move to more open areas, often to drink, and after foraging all morning they find an area of denser cover for a mid-day doze before commencing feeding.

Both types of partridge can be difficult to observe during the summer, when plant cover renders them invisible as they furtively search for their food. Using a car as a hide, they can sometimes be watched on roadside verges, usually in pairs, picking and scratching for fragments of vegetation as they gently pass their morning like a pair of pensioners out for a Sunday stroll, weary of the world, but somehow a little wiser.

SCRUBLAND WARBLERS

If partridges are weary pensioners, Grasshopper Warblers *Locustella naevia* are the punk rockers, loaded with the musical equipment to produce a mindless and monotonous sonic blast that perforates summer scrubland. This racket is typically delivered towards the end of a drizzly evening and is of such a high pitch that many older naturalists may be quite unable to hear it. In the past these birds were associated with damp sedge marshes, Osier beds and bushy reeded areas, but providing the habitat structure is suitable they can turn up almost anywhere. Thus, from the end of April through to mid-May, the dry, thick and tangled growth of scrub encroached downland is a good place to search for them. But, I am afraid, like Nightingales they are almost ridiculously skulking and often seem quite good at throwing their voices. Getting a decent view of one can be hard work but it is worth persisting because, despite their drab colouring, they are neatly marked birds. They are only one of a number of such warblers that visit the scrub in summer to feed and breed.

The Whitethroat *Sylvia communis* is probably the bird that is most readily found and identified because in spring the male is easily the most rowdy lad in the bushes. His vigorous panicking rattle is almost continually, and certainly cheerfully, poured out of any tiny clearing between the briars. This territorial boasting goes on all summer because in most years two broods are reared from an untidy grass dish built in the lower fronds of the vegetation. If not singing they are always scolding, and the characteristic repeated *Tcheck ... Tcheck ... Tchecking* will soon lead you to your bird. Once you get a glimpse of one you will see they are dishevelled restless little warblers, constantly hopping amongst the undergrowth, cocking their tails and waving their pale grey crests.

Towards the woody end of scrub development Blackcaps *Sylvia atricapilla* become more abundant as they need higher song posts, usually in trees, than the Whitethroats. Their song is as loud as a Blackbird's, but also very similar to their scrubland co-habitant, the Garden Warbler *Sylvia borin*. If anything the Blackcap is louder and clearer whilst the Garden Warbler produces longer phrases with a tendency to grate, rather like the Whitethroat. Of course, this information is meaningless to all those who have not yet spent ages peering into the shade, training their ears to pick out the peculiarities of each song. Such a talent, once developed, is very useful, not only allowing you to save time identifying a known species but also in that any new, possibly rare, warbler sounds so different that you cannot miss it. (Being able to nonchalantly identify some hidden song without even raising your binoculars is an added bonus that will never cease to irritate your birding friends.) Both of these species are elegant birds, designed with smooth curves and coloured with simple earthy tones. The Gar-

den Warbler is strictly a summer visitor and returns to Africa between September and May. The Blackcap though can be found overwintering, even turning up on suburban bird tables. This habit is apparently a recent development as it has only really been observed in the last twenty years. As British breeding birds migrate south in autumn they are replaced by those which breed in northern and eastern Europe. Blackcaps are omnivorous and survive by feeding on wild berries until these stocks dwindle and, in harsher weather they look for our offerings of fat, bread and cheese. Despite the more precarious nature of this habit there is undoubtedly a benefit to overwintering as far north as possible. Namely that these birds will have a shorter distance to travel back to their summer breeding territories. On a first-come, first-served basis, these tougher Blackcaps will be more likely to start the breeding season as territory holders and therefore be more successful than their fellows who sunned themselves in southern Europe or Africa.

The desire to fly south is easy to understand because away from the scrub the wide slopes of downland can be desperately desolate places in winter. There may be only a total of 35 individual birds spread over each square kilometre, mostly Rooks *Corvus frugilegus* and Starlings *Sturnus vulgaris*. Others may move into the scrubby areas to roost and here Woodpigeons *Columba palumbus*, Linnets, Redpolls *Carduelis flammea*, Greenfinches *Chloris chloris*, Chaffinches, Bramblings *Fringilla montifringilla* and House Sparrows *Passer domesticus* form low density populations, whilst the occasional solitary visiting Great Grey Shrike *Lanius excubitor*, Hen Harrier *Circus cyaneus*, or Short-eared Owl *Asio flammeus* suffers the meteorological might of winter out on the barren escarpment.

Life may be tough on the grassland in winter, but there is one predator which is present all year round, although I'd wait for a summer's evening to look for it.

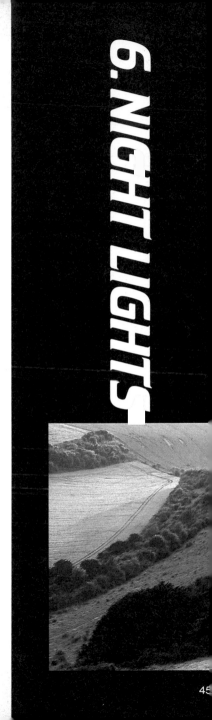

As the light perishes, all colour decays. The vibrant greens of the hummocks of Hawthorns blend with the dulling striations of the grass tussocks. The yellow of the Rock-rose, the powder blue of the Harebells and the pastel hue of thousands of Milkwort flowers all suffuse into a palette of milky grey. Perspectives are crushed by the ensuing darkness, all form is reduced and the landscape becomes soft and simplified, as if an Orientalist had suddenly dissolved into an Impressionist dirge. Human vision is poor, but the senses of taste and smell explode in effectiveness. The taste of sweet grass is on your lips and you can smell night prowling in. That pure cold smell, slightly wet, tainted with vegetation, but full of inky blue and pale distant planets. A smell of was-warm, is-still and will-be-sharp.

As positive becomes monochrome negative, movement too evaporates. Sounds sharpen and cut across early mists, Moorhens bicker one more time from a distant dew pond, a Pheasant barks from the other side of the earth and a few billion insects buzz monotonously in a synthesised track of the inane. Ghost moths bounce over the canopies of grass, dropping their eggs into the volumes below and then strafe away into fuzzy forests of thistles.

THE BARN OWL

Finally, as a reprieve from this decline in perceptual reality, a flashing grey light appears jinking and jiggling, sometimes pulsing in intensity. It arches over the fields, toppling over the bubbly smoke-scape of the Hawthorn thickets and as it nears it begins to flare, to flash white like a burning magnesium kite fixed to the sky with elastic. It rises up, stalls and then falters forwards staggering through the vacuum without sound. It flinches, turns on its axis, realigns, re-floats and renews its purposeful exploration of the air. Then it

LEFT **Barn Owl**
RIGHT **Hunting grounds**

twists, implodes and plummets into a patch of grey-green. After a second, the Barn Owl *Tyto alba* re-inflates and rises up in a rapid careering flurry, back-tracking more directly than in its former lazy loafings. It has snatched a quiet mammal and is delivering it to its brood of barn-held and hungry young.

On examination, these heinous compositions of feather and fury, are surely the most ugly owlets of all. Long faced and pocked with down, they are like zombie birds, back from the dead, and their mentality matches. On first approach to their sordid nesting ledge they hiss like punctured psychopaths. Then they rock from side to side in a primitive voodoo dance, head down, breathing out a dry, prolonged pant of stale vole breath. At the 'fingers too close for comfort' stage they erupt in an untidy morass of ragged wings, flailing talons and clouds of feather talcum. This musty powder is made of the preened and broken waxy feather-sheaths; sharp pointed quills, which provide initial protection for each feather. The top of this is pecked off and the feather slowly emerges from its 'pin'. If the base of the tube is still bloody then the feather is still growing and is sensitive to damage but when all the dandruff is preened and fluffed away the base of the quill hardens and dies leaving the feather in a fit state to take to the air. At this stage the owls move up a dance class. Now when disturbed they spread their wings in an upturned semi-circle and tip them forwards in a successful attempt to appear as large as possible. When six angry owlets so perform, they metamorphose into a sextet of headdresses fit for a New Guinea King.

Despite a sad and continuing decline over much of Britain, the Barn Owl can still be seen floating about over areas of grassland searching for its prey, principally small mammals. In summer, with a brood of hungry young, they may start to hunt at half past six or seven o'clock in the evening sunlight, although they are principally a nocturnal species, complete with all the adaptations such a lifestyle requires.

Their eyes are considerably smaller than those of most owls in relation to their body size, but they are nevertheless extremely effective in bad light. The cornea and lens are huge compared to the human eye and this results in a smaller image being focused on the retina, which is very near the front of the eye. Consequently very little light is lost between entering the eye and striking the extremely sensitive photoreceptive cells, the rod and cone cells, which cover the retina. The rod cells are the most sensitive of the two in low light, but permit only black and white vision. Up to 56,000 of these rod cells are spread over one square millimetre of the bird's eye, and many of these individual cells are linked with each other by tiny nerves so that light sensitivity is enhanced at very low intensities. Cone cells, which produce colour vision, are of little use in darkness, but are nevertheless abundant in the owl's eye, to allow increased detail at times when colour vision is feasible. Another specialisation of improved sight is the presence of an unusually powerful muscle which acts on the lens and cornea to maintain a sharp focus on the owl's intended prey. In fact this muscle is so strong that strengthening plates known as 'scleral ossicles' are arranged around the periphery of the cornea to protect the eye from being pulled apart by its own muscular activity. This super-strengthening results in the eyes being well locked into the skull, and because they face forward the owl's field of view is only about 110°, 70 per cent of which can be seen by both eyes at once, so-called binocular vision. Not being able to see behind it is not a problem because the owl can twist its head through nearly 360° using its long flexible neck to see behind itself. Binocular vision allows an object to be viewed from slightly different angles and this enables the owl's brain to judge distances very accurately, a vital skill in a hunter.

Owls supplement this optical adaptation by some extremely comical behaviour.

They continually bob and weave their heads from side to side, sometimes even twisting upside-down or sideways, always staring at the object of their mad attention. This allows them to compare the relative movement of other points around the object on which they are focused and produces an even more precise positioning of this in space. All bad news if you are a vole under scrutiny.

Barn Owls also have extraordinarily acute hearing. Their 'humanesque' facial disc is made up of two enormous ear conches. A ruff of unusually dense feathers emerges from a ridge of skin and produces a mat of material as near impermeable to sound as possible, whilst within the familiar heart shaped face, are thin, light, filamentous feathers, readily permeable to any sound. Together, these form a highly developed sonic reflector, much more than just a pretty face. The actual openings to the ears are situated asymmetrically, that is with one lower and one higher in respect to a median line drawn between the owl's eyes. This is the key to the owl's advanced hearing.

In a series of experiments conducted at Cornell University in the United States, a number of Barn Owls were placed in a large completely dark room. They were observed, using an infra-red viewing device, and it was found that the owls were able to locate and capture their prey using their hearing alone. Further, they were able to discern the direction it was travelling, and align their talons for maximum capture efficiency whilst audio-tracking their prey in complete darkness. In further experiments, the sound of a vole was simulated by loudspeakers hidden beneath the sandy floor. As soon as the owls took to the wing, the sound source was switched off and the owls were forced to strike at where they could remember the sound arising from. This gave rise to an increased frequency of misses, but misses of only plus or minus 0.5 to 0.3 of a degree. If the owls were allowed to hear the sound for a brief moment once they had taken to the air,

their capture success rose to an almost invariable 100 per cent.

The asymmetry of the owl's ears not only provides it with an extremely accurate method of judging distance, but also causes sounds of particular frequencies to reach each ear at different intensities. Using this difference the owl is able to construct three-dimensional sensitivity patterns, which enable it to know when it is directly facing the source of the sound. Indeed when analysing slow motion film of Cornell's Barn Owls hunting, it was seen that they approached the prey looking straight at it and at the last moment, when about a metre from the target, suddenly thrust their feet forward until they almost touch their beaks. In the same instant they pull their heads backwards out of the way so that the head, which had been on a precise collision course with the prey, is effectively replaced by a spiny cage of primed talons. This dangerously efficient targeting system is further perfected by the owls' ability to wiggle their ears. Built into the bases of their ear flaps are a series of especially well-developed muscles which have probably evolved to enable the owls to move parts of their auditory apparatus to change and intensify the sensitivity patterns which they can receive. I have no doubt that the American Owls can blow smoke rings and have been recruited by the CIA for 'special nocturnal duties'.

With hearing being so important to the hunting owl it is not surprising that Barn Owls should be capable of slow, gentle and, above all, silent flight. They achieve all three by having a very large wing area in relation to their weight. Thus, the bird can fly very slowly, without stalling, and has no need for powerful, potentially noisy, wingstrokes. Silence is further ensured by the construction of the owl's feathers. The upper-side of the flight feathers is coated in a velvety pile which is produced by the prolonged hairy ends of the tiny barbules which link the vanes in each feather. In addition to this, the ends of the barbs along the leading edges of the primary feathers form a neat comb which smooths out and silences the flow of air over the wings. This reduces flying efficiency, but because speed is unimportant to the precision of the Barn Owl, this is of little disadvantage. Further, it seems that Barn Owls have eliminated any ultrasonic noise from the sound of their wing-beats, which is important as most of their small mammal prey are very sensitive to this frequency.

Whilst the aesthetic marvel of one of these buoyant ghosts flapping low over the ground, rising and falling, gracefully gliding and clipping the grass heads is enough to evoke a dream sequence in any naturalist's night, for once visualise it as a machine. The solid living material made of carbon, hydrogen and oxygen, of fats, proteins and a host of compounds that are all bound together with such diabolical precision. Designed over eons of time, by the selection of tiny errors, by the competition of millions of lives. A product of perfection.

The owl has vanished and darkness grips the grassland. Another predator sorties forth, stepping softly. Black and dull, a fox, once the colour of sunset rust, is now smoke in the moonlight. He wears the softest paw and puts it everywhere. From the back of the gasworks, to the garden shed, from the Cow Parsley bed to the shadows of the oak and along the dusty farm track.

THE FOX

His tracks lace up the Thames, the Mersey and the Tyne. His voice is heard from Westminster Cathedral to Stonehenge. Paperboys smell his scent from Torquay to Tarbet. He is fed, fancied, loved, loathed, blasted, snared and chased; at worst he is worn. He is mystery and magic. And on a summer's evening, through a mist of pollen, when his flanks glow like embers, his chin like fresh snow and his eyes like gems – then, he is magnificent.

Over much of grass and scrubland the Red Fox *Vulpes vulpes* is our principal predator. Describing its diet is impossible because it will eat almost anything

Fox

depending on its occurrence and abundance in each particular fox's home range. Silver paper, sausage wrappers and even elastic bands have been recovered from stomach or faecal analysis, so foxes are more than just carnivores. Foxes hunt without having a single species of prey in mind; they are opportunists. They use their sight, hearing and smell to find non-specific prey with equal effectiveness. But despite the diversity of their diet small mammals almost invariably form the largest component. There is no specialised physiological adaptation to such predation, as there is in the Barn Owl. Instead, foxes use their sight for hunting in daylight, and hearing and smell for their night-time prowling. They walk upwind, stopping and head turning to listen for voles rustling or chewing in the grass. Once located the prey is pursued intently. In long grass, foxes 'mouse-pounce', leaping up in a pretty bound to see their fleeing prey over the screen of stems. Often if they miss with the first strike they pounce again and again, bouncing about like rubber balls. Such leaping may also serve to pinpoint the sound of the animal more precisely by providing two points of focus, rather like the owl bobbing its head.

Adult foxes need 350 to 550 grams of food per day, which is a lot of voles, so rabbits are often chosen as a more profitable prey source. These may be pursued in daylight, often by bolting into the middle of a warren to send the startled occupants reeling underground. Nearly always unsuccessful the fox then zig-zags about the warren hoping that one insane bunny will re-emerge to graze at its burrow entrance. In fact the daft rabbits often do just this, and the fox seizes a victim with apparent arrogance. This brash behaviour is probably the result of the ineffectiveness of stalking rabbits in daylight. When above ground in large numbers, the array of rabbits' ears, noses and eyes are such a good early warning system that the fox is rarely successful. The one other diurnal ploy is to dig out juvenile rabbits from shallow earths on the edge of the warren. At night however, the tables turn and when rabbits stray hundreds of metres away from the warren to graze, a lone fox that sneaks upwind is more than likely to be a first time winner. In the wake of myxomatosis, with rabbit populations down by 90 per cent, there has been no catalogued decline in fox numbers or reduction in their survival. A further indication that these highly successful predators always land on their feet.

As the fox's dusty shadow bounces into oblivion down the dim grey track, a million holes are pricked into the roof of the world. Cool has become cold and a hundred tiny twinklings sparkle on the bankside as if some of those constellations had slipped and tumbled into the tangled matrix of grasses. Fairy lights, static sparks of bright white light. The grass stars are shining.

GLOW-WORMS

Down in the dungeons, in a weird world of towering columns, still air and the damp smell of fungus, where the sounds of voles chewing, ants marching, and roots pushing into the soil do little to reduce the monotony of the downland metropolis, a small insect wriggles. Wingless, dull brown, small eyed and with yellowish legs she wanders up the grass stem, surely the most dowdy and ugly larval-like girl in the grassland. Carefully negotiating a sleeping Cinnabar Moth, she ascends to a point clear to the night air, twists her tail skyward and ignites.

From dreary to the most famous beetle in the world. In a single flicker the female Glow-worm *Lampyris noctiluca* lights her torches of desire and becomes a living lantern, a nymphomaniac neon, a street walking streetlight plying her femininity to attract a mate. But of course she has attracted more than her mate. She has illuminated the imagination of poets since the birth of history. The Greeks called her the 'Bright tailed', Fabre 'a spark fallen from the moon', and Wordsworth 'the earthborn-star'. The Glow-worm is undoubtedly my favourite insect, and one

which can be easily found on grassy slopes, hedge banks, heaths and wasteland in June and July throughout southern England. All you need is a little darkness.

Glow-worms are truly self-luminous insects. They are not phosphorescent. Phosphorescence is caused by the emission of a light which has previously been absorbed from exterior radiations. The female Glow-worm actually has light-producing organs in the last three divisions of her body. Here, the insect's translucent cuticle overlays a photogenic organ consisting of a transparent outer layer, known as the photogen layer, and an inner reflective layer. This reflecting layer consists of a milky coating of microscopic urate crystals which serve to prevent wasteful internal absorption and to reflect the light outwards. The photogen layer produces the light using a chemical reaction. A compound called luciferin is combined with oxygen, that is, oxidised, to form oxyluciferin. This reaction is dependent on a supply of water and oxygen, and consequently the photogenic organ is smothered with a complex arrangement of filamentous air-tubes which supply its demands for air.

The pyrotechnic display is under the full control of the beetle and is only operated during the chosen hours of darkness. It is, of course, a highly specialised form of sexual attraction. The wingless, and consequently flightless, female needs to advertise herself to the over-active airborne males. These males are much more like typical beetles. Equipped with working wings and elytra, they have a pitch-like coloration, a yellow-sided thorax and comparatively gigantic eyes, with which they no doubt locate their glowing mates. This pretty luminescence is not the Glow-worm's only biological claim to fame, because the larvae exhibit a quite fascinating form of feeding behaviour.

The larval Glow-worm is carnivorous, feeding almost exclusively on snails. The prey victimised range from cherry-sized Banded Snails *Cepaea* spp. up to large Garden Snails *Helix aspersa*, and all are immobilised with an extraordinarily delicate deftness by the patient larvae. The Glow-wormette is armed with a sharp slender hook constructed from a highly specialised pair of mandibles. Using this hair-like tool the insect repeatedly taps gently on the snail's soft and sticky mantle or foot. There is no aggression, no stabbing, just a delicate touching and tweaking of the snail. There is no hurry and usually a brief rest between each kiss, until about half a dozen have been delivered. The insect's toxin is remarkably rapid and after a few malignant spasms the snail becomes a limp bucket of meat entirely at the mercy of the Glow-worm. What follows is a vile feasting on the living mollusc by one or more larvae, because often, as soon as the snail is immobilised, a number of Glow-worm larvae guests rush to the side of the 'soup bowl' and stick in their 'straws'. This is a precise analogy because the larvae lack any chewing apparatus. Instead they inject an enzyme which dissolves the solid flesh into liquid soup. This is then drawn back through a slender canal on the base of the insect's hook and into its stomach. What is amazing is that this whole operation may carry on some way up a stalk of grass where the snail has attached itself. If the larva's initial attack was any more aggressive, the struggling snail could dislodge itself and fall to the safety of the ground below. Instead the entire operation is a gently executed feat, aided by a small sticky organ on the insect's abdomen. This tiny rosette is made up of a number of thin fleshy fingers which stick firmly onto the grass stem or snail shell in order to steady the consumer. This device is also used for cleaning, and after a full meal of snail gruel the larvae meticulously groom themselves before disappearing down into the grass. Here, like the adults, they hide during the day, safe from the bills of birds but at the mercy of the sniffling snouts of our shrews.

LEFT **Glow-worm**

Oh for the nose of a shrew. Taut, prehensile, and ever probing, they are adorned with a pair of tactile fans, each a complex of delicate supersensitive antennae. These whiskers shroud the shrew's head in a matrix of movable sensor points, quivering to a blur around the two tiny eyes, which are lost above its velvety cheeks. The enamelled pin-head eyes are doubtlessly poor in resolution, but that nose, and those whiskers, must be worth a hundred of our pink fleshy protuberances and tatty drooping moustaches. They are pushed into every damp cleft in the undergrowth, up every hollow, down every crack at a furious pace, eagerly sniffing out insect delights.

When I was young I once pretended that I was a shrew. Running around insanely, jamming my head into every corner, constantly discovering food and eating it at a hectic pace, then tearing off in search of more. After a few seconds' activity, I'd lie down and pretend to sleep. Then, I'd burst back into life and begin to forage again. I could only ever maintain this pace for a few minutes and the odd digestive biscuits I devoured could never have kept me going any longer. My fascination for shrews continued into later life. Their mania, the way they seem to exist in a different time continuum, where everything happens at super speed, so obsessed me that on my twenty-second Christmas Day, I forsook all festivities and spent my time catching, feeding and observing my most dynamic friends, the shrews.

My childhood impersonations of shrews were remarkably accurate because these mammals are exceedingly active both day and night, for about ten periods with shorter rest periods in between. This intense activity is governed by an exceedingly high metabolic rate. Weighing in at only 8 grams, a shrew uses 36 calories of energy per gram every hour it lives (in comparison a man uses about 2 calories per gram per hour), because of

LEFT **The grassland undertaker**

their small volume and thus relatively large surface area. The upshot of this phenomenon is that shrews need to eat three quarters of their own body weight a day and thus we must expect them to have a feeding strategy to ensure their survival. In scientific terms we would expect them to 'optimally forage'.

The use, or misuse, of the term 'optimal' is currently fashionable and rife in the field of behavioural ecology, being applied to every strategy from foraging to mating, in every species from crabs to midges. By definition, optimal means 'most favourable' so in this case it refers to the most favourable method of finding, catching and consuming the most nutritious foodstuffs. The rationale for the concept of optimal foraging develops from the premise that animals need to harvest their food efficiently, a result of evolutionary pressures generated both within and between species which lead to intense competition. Natural selection should favour individuals who are the best equipped to deal with this competition. Seemingly short term objectives, such as feeding behaviour, may have highly influential effects on eventual reproductive success: through efficient food gathering an individual spends a shorter time looking for sustenance and has more time to devote to territory maintenance, mating and essential resting. To increase foraging efficiency to an optimal level may involve maximising the amount and calorific value of the food eaten, maximising a specific type of nutrient required, or minimising any fluctuations in the overall intake over a period of time. Of course, there is more to a shrew's life than just foraging. Competition for time and energy must occur between this and other facets of its behaviour such as resting and mating. Indeed, even within the strategy of foraging there are sub-divisions such as types of food, places to hunt and search paths to locate the food and to consider these separately may lead to an apparent optimisation of each. In the real lives of these tiny tearaways all of these components are closely integrated and we must only expect an overall, perhaps long term, maximising of the individual's fitness. That is the theory, now consider yourself a shrew. In order to breed and then keep your family healthy you must choose which shops to go to, which foods to take off the shelf at which costs, how often to visit the shop and how much time you spend searching for, purchasing, preparing and finally eating your food. In the winter of 1982 I decided to discover just how shrews went shopping.

There are over 100 species of shrew worldwide, but in Britain we only have three species. The Water Shrew *Neomys fodiens*, is the largest and is not an inhabitant of grasslands. It favours the banks of clear, unpolluted streams and ponds wherever there is thick cover. The latter requirement is also essential for the presence of our other two species, the Pygmy Shrew *Sorex minutus*, and the Common Shrew *S. araneus*, both of which can be found in dense populations in our rough grasslands. In the past shrews have proved difficult to keep in captivity and even the great behaviourist, Konrad Lorenz failed to maintain the health of shrews in his care. Realising that I would need hungry, healthy shrews, I chose the larger of the two available species, the Common Shrew, for my studies. These plain chocolate-brown chaps are quite common bustling and busily exploring the burrows and tunnels, threading through the litter and soils, of the landscape. On many cold winter's mornings, I set my traps, baited with blowfly pupae (casters), under clods of earth and amongst thick grass and bushy shrubs on some local derelict water meadows. I returned to these at least twice a day to ensure the survival of any captives and removed those caught to a battery of vivaria set up in my garage. Each of these cosy little hotels was fully fitted out with a lower level of deciduous leaf-litter and an upper layer of warm dry grass. The shrews were amply provided with a diet of crickets, mealworms

A shrew in a bottle – doomed

and casters. All of my guests had separate accommodation because these somewhat sweet little animals can also be remarkably aggressive and may even fight to the death. Every night, in preparation for my tests I would deny a party of the shrews food for six hours, not long enough to starve them but just long enough to ensure their hunger. As soon as my mother had cleared away the tea, I placed a large covered tray on the dining room table and filled it with an array of suitable foods. Mealworms, crickets, earthworms and casters were all weighed and their precise energy values determined before the famished shrews were allowed to make their essential choices. Then, in the weak glow of a red safe-light, armed with a battery of stopwatches, my girlfriend and I recorded how long it took each shrew to discover each prey item, how long it then took to eat it, and how long it was before it chose another of the four prey items provided. These trials continued throughout the winter and finally bored all of my family rigid.

By early spring I had conducted hundreds of tests and measured parameters not only relating to the shrews foraging, but also as diverse as the proportion of water in earthworms, the speed at which crickets could hop across my choice chamber, the differences in food value between crickets' legs and abdomens, the relative ease with which each prey type could be seen. Finally using all of these, I developed some highly accurate theoretical decision rules for my shrews and compared these to their real behaviour.

The results were quite alarming. Within a single type of diet, the shrews successfully selected the greatest proportion of the most beneficial items in the most beneficial order of consumption. Even more astounding were the results obtained when the shrews were faced with a choice of all four diets at once. In these tests they were found to concentrate disproportionately on the more profitable prey items. Even at incredibly low densities of the profitable items, they would ignore the others and actively search out the best meals. All in all, my furtive little friends were behaving as super predators.

Of course, tests conducted in a box on a dining table in Southampton may not stand precise comparison with shrews' behaviour out on the downlands of southern England. However, evidence resulting from observations of wild shrews does actually compare favourably with my own. By studying the composition of the shrews' diet through analysis of their faeces and comparing it to the various insect densities caught in the wild, other workers have discovered that the shrews do seem to have concentrated on the more favourable prey items and especially so at times when they were in greater abundance. This suggests that shrews may develop a search image, a behavioural trait which enables them to find a single type of prey even more effectively than they otherwise would. Other scientists have examined the actual method of foraging and prey detection and found that a search image for a certain prey is rapidly generated and also that the tactile and auditory senses were exceptionally advanced, as befits this highly specialised insectivorous super predator. In the dim light of my dining room I could not help but marvel at the extraordinary subtlety that these tiny animals exhibit. To think of them, outside, hidden under the hummocks of grass, each performing as near optimally as it can in a desperate bid to survive whilst we bumble about, making inept and dangerous decisions which would, in a less forgiving world, produce disastrous consequences. I no longer amble about in a state of ambivalence when I go shopping. I always attempt to follow my nose straight to the shelf where my most optimal items can be found, more often than not and questionably, chocolate biscuits!

GRASSLAND UNDERTAKERS

Whilst perusing the summer scrub it is always interesting to discover a corpse. That of a mouse, vole, or shrew of course!

Approach it stealthily, with gentle footsteps, kneel down with your nose as close as its state of decay permits, and rapidly flick it over. With any luck you will see an infuriated pair of black and orange banded burying beetles scurrying away.

There are at least eight British undertaking beetles although most of these are uncommon and have localised and southern distributions. Up to 60 or more beetles also frolic amongst carrion but do not warrant the title of burying beetle: only those of the genus *Nicrophorus* exhibit this funereal expertise. *Nicrophorus humator* is a massive common beetle, which may exceed 5 centimetres in length. Its body is entirely black, having no orange markings on the elytra, but the terminal club at the tip of its antennae is marked with a reddish-yellow. The head and thorax are in fact shiny, but the heavy sculpturing of the body plates makes the beetle appear dull. Discovering one of these on your hands and knees under the corpse of a small mammal or bird is a startling experience, rather like coming face to face with a Coleopteran dinosaur!

I have only ever seen one of these imposing insects, but the burying beetles marked with orange bands on their back plates are generally far more common. There are two species likely to be encountered, *Nicrophorus vespilloides* and *Nicrophorus investigator*. These are largely black, robust-looking insects with strong, thick-set legs, clumpy thoraxes, heads and antennae, and an overall compact and graceless structure. They are not unattractive, but it is their extraordinary behaviour and life history that makes them interesting.

Their sense of smell is obviously acute and enables them to rapidly locate any carrion, onto which they subsequently converge using a powerful flight. Should a male arrive first at the graveside he begins feeding by chewing a small hole in the side or underside flesh of the corpse. After a short while, if he remains the only undertaker in attendance he will climb to an elevated position on top of the carrion, or a nearby insect high point, and begin to emit a powerful pheromone. Raising his abdomen obliquely, his head down supporting his upheld body, he sprays the air with this chemical attractant in order to recruit a mate. The smell of the carrion may, of course, attract other burying beetles of the same sex, and to a degree these are tolerated until a female finally appears. Now some serious macho-male fighting breaks out, the result of which is that only one male and one female beetle remain at the corpse. It is here that their courtship and mating takes place and the eggs are deposited. The cadavering couple skulk under the carcass and begin to excavate the earth, pushing it to the side using their robust limbs and cutting all obstacles, such as grass roots, away using their mandibles. Slowly but surely the dead animal sinks into the earth until it is completely covered. If the corpse has been inconsiderate enough to die in a place where the ground is unsuitable for excavation, these beetles have even been seen dragging it to an area where their digging will be easier. Soon the carcass disappears and is entombed between 2 and 7 centimetres below ground in a neat mortuary cellar. Once this room is completed the beetles use their mandibles to strip the skin of feathers, or fur, and this forms a dense carpet on the floor of the chamber. Next, the female digs a narrow horizontal passage and lays several eggs at intervals, each in a pocket made with her ovipositor. Now, with the eggs safely stashed in the dark catacomb, the female suddenly turns on her mate and hurriedly drives him away from the burrow. She returns, climbs to the top of the carrion, and in the humid and stinking darkness, makes a small circular crater in the corpse and begins to feed. Until now she has been so diligently working that she has eaten little.

The larvae emerge in five days and immediately burrow through the soil or follow the passage towards their waiting meal. All finally gather on the top of the corpse at the crater gnawed by the female, attracted by the now powerful odour and her noisy stridulations. They appear to touch the carrion with their mouthparts, but in fact wait for the female to serve them with her own. Her mandibles are flexed open and a drop of brown liquid is fed in turn to each larva. They wrestle like piglets over a sow's teat, struggling, rolling and pushing each other to obtain this predigested food, the more persistent even scrambling up the parent's legs in order to reach the droplet. Fortunately for the female, within a few hours her offspring are capable of feeding themselves and are only dependent upon her again for short periods after their first and second moults. These moults drastically change the appearance of the larvae. They begin well, segmented, bulbous and legged in appearance, but curiously become more primitive and larviform, until by their third moult they are almost maggot-like. In a few days each larva bores horizontally through the wall of the chamber and up to thirty centimetres into the surrounding soil. Here the body begins to rotate about its longest axis and after several hours spinning forms a pupa. About a fortnight later an adult beetle emerges.

It is worth noting that burying beetles are not wholly carrion feeders and that they will feed on the many blowfly larvae which may infest the carcasses. There is in fact a whole group of beetles, as many as 50 species of which are native to Britain, known as carrion beetles. These feed on fly or other carrion feeding insect larvae. Most are small, rounded and black and are often found with burying beetles.

The rich variety of vegetation on downland provides well for an equally rich array of herbivorous invertebrates. The snails are well represented; the banded snails Cepaea hortensis and C. nemoralis are always common, whilst at least 30–40 other species occur. Some, such as Hellicella itala, even sliming over the warmest, driest slopes. Woodlice swell these saprophagous ranks, feeding on dead or senescent vegetation, whilst millions of ants play a significant role in the ecology of the whole habitat. Their hills bury the original turf and end up supporting a unique flora of their own, many plant species being imported as seeds by the foraging workers. Spider and bug species are also numerous but not so typical of the grassland environment as the grasshoppers and crickets.

THE OVERLOOKED ORTHOPTERA

The British grasshoppers are greatly under-watched, under-recorded and under-rated by the amateur naturalist. It was only in 1920 that the first monograph on the British Orthoptera was published, and not until 1965 that a field guide for the layman was produced. Amongst a host of badger fiends, bird fanatics and butterfly aficionados, I know of no one with a similar obsession for grasshoppers.

In truth, our Orthopteran fauna is rather poor compared to that of similar latitudes in Europe. The continental climate, with its warmer, drier summers, provides for a much greater species diversity. Affinity for warmth and sunshine leads to a similar diversity in southern England though, and here there are up to 40 species, 30 native and 10 introduced. East Anglia and Central England hold between 25 and 30 species but north of a line from the Wirral to the Humber there may only be 18, north of Edinburgh only 10, and, not surprisingly, on the Scottish Islands, only 3 very hardy grasshoppers hop.

Grasshoppers select south-facing slopes, for increased warmth and shelter, and any small hollow in a hill-side acting as a suntrap may attract the greatest numbers. Scuffing about in such a spot soon sends browny blurs bounding around in all directions, the insects occasionally breaking into flight. The leaping powers of grasshoppers are well known. They are equipped with gross tibial muscles in the femurs of their enlarged hind-legs. These 'drumsticks' are crammed with muscles, each attached to the femoral walls in the

spaces between the fishbone ridges which characteristically appear on the sides of the hind-legs. On contracting, these powerful tissues forcibly straighten out the slender tibia and effectively catapult the insect into the air. Once airborne they adopt a floating posture, legs spread wide, to stabilise the body and further ensure that they land on their feet. Observing this particular behaviour in the field is impossible but a little time watching the habits of the Common Green Grasshopper *Omocestus viridulus*, the Meadow Grasshopper *Chorthippus parallelus* or the Common Field Grasshopper *C. brunneus* is time well spent. Indeed the ignorance surrounding this group of insects is somewhat puzzling because of their relatively large size. Some, such as the Mole Cricket *Gryllotalpa gryllotalpa* and Great Green Bush-cricket *Tettigonia viridissima*, are often over 5 centimetres long and rank among the largest of all British insects. They are also some of the most exciting.

The Great Green Bush-cricket is a brilliant green, raucous insect which can be found quite commonly along the coastal grasslands of southern England. Its high-pitched, harsh song comprises a series of long bursts, punctuated by barely noticeable hesitations, giving a similar sound effect to a continuous synthesiser gone madly out of control on feed-back mode. It is delivered by the male, usually from the higher parts of vegetation; its favourite song sites being thistles. Despite their large size, bright coloration and extraordinary song, Great Greens can be almost impossible to see. Their straggly shape and brown stripe, which runs the length of their back, serves to break up their outline amongst the vegetation. You can be stood staring at the source of the intolerable racket but never actually see it.

Whilst the Great Green Bush-cricket can be found in most shrubby areas, along hedgerows, in thistles, nettles, brambles, bracken or gorse beds, the Mole Cricket is a rarity in Britain. In recent years it has only been recorded from isolated areas of southern England, and most recently from the water meadows and flood plains around Chichester. In Europe, however, it is common, especially in the south where it frequents the vicinity of rivers, streams, canals or ponds. It is a huge insect, overall brown in colour with its fore-legs massively modified for digging. It is somewhat surprisingly covered with a fine velvety hair. Its forewings only cover a half of the abdomen, and there is often a tendency for individuals to be lighter underneath.

As its name implies the Mole Cricket spends much of its life in underground burrows, the depth of which depends to a great extent on the moisture content of the soil: the less moisture the deeper the burrow. This chamber is a quite remarkable piece of engineering, not through its size or craftsmanship but because of its extraordinary design which amplifies, channels and enhances the cricket's song. It has two openings, each of a diameter which is one third of the wavelength of the sound the cricket produces. This proportion is the scientific optimum for maximum efficiency in any loudspeaker. The openings taper back to form two symmetrical horns which close on a channel where the singing insect occupies a constriction which fits neatly around its neck. The horns of the burrow are used in the same way as those found on gramophones, which were necessary before modern transistorised amplifiers made any degree of efficiency unnecessary. Interference between the soundwaves emitted by each of the horns concentrates the sound in the insect's head to tail plane so that very little sound energy is wasted. The sound intensity generated by the cricket in its home-made loudspeaker reaches 90 decibels, the same intensity of sound as that that can be heard 15 metres away from a heavy truck or pneumatic drill. Not surprisingly Mole Crickets can be detected from over 600 metres.

On warm evenings and nights from mid-April onwards the Mole Cricket's long churring bursts sound over the grassy scrub of the Mediterranean. The actual sound itself is made in a similar fashion to running a finger over the teeth of a comb. The crickets have veins projecting upwards from their fore-wings which act as scrapers. On the undersides of their opposite fore-wings they have toothed files. The sound is made with the wings lifted a little from the surface of the body where they are vibrated so that the left scraper runs over the right file. It slides over easily on the opening stroke, because of the direction of the teeth, but on the closing stroke the teeth catch and make both wings vibrate, each closing stroke playing over 30 teeth in just 8.5 milliseconds. A central section of the wing, known as the 'harp', has a resonant frequency which equals the sound frequency produced by the scraping and combing of the wings and this panel acts as a loudspeaker, in fact as a pre-speaker for the acoustically superb burrows.

Unfortunately, this exciting insect is unlikely to be encountered in the British Isles, as is our second largest true cricket, the Field Cricket *Gryllus campestris*. This large rotund shiny black insect has probably never been common. It uses its large mandibles to dig a burrow about 20 cm long and here, from early May onwards, males can be found singing. However, stealthy approach is needed, because once disturbed they produce a loud, audible click as they snap their fore-wings together and then retreat rapidly into their cave. Their vigilant nature normally makes them difficult to catch, but if they can be kept from the safety of their burrows their flightless weak jumpings allow them to be caught.

Field Crickets make excellent pets and in the past were sold for this purpose in many parts of southern Europe. Recent research reveals that this species is now limited to two sites in southern England, the best of which, almost unbelievably, is situated on a cricket pitch. I wonder if enough remain to field a team?

The English chalk has always been important economically. It has been quarried since Roman times and in the Middle Ages was taken, in enormous quantities, from Thameside to East Anglia and Essex to replenish the essential nutrients needed for agriculture in these areas. Harder chalk was sometimes chosen for building and could be ornately carved, as seen in the vaulted ceilings of Arundel Castle and Chichester Cathedral. More recently chalk has been burned to produce mortar and agricultural lime and is consumed on a massive scale in the manufacture of cement. Indeed good quality chalk is considered so valuable in some places that it is transported miles to the actual cement works. However, such uses are secondary to the most important, which has always been farming.

During Norman times a system of sheep folding was developed. Western, Old Wiltshire or Old Hampshire sheep were kept in pens on arable land by day, and put out on the down by night. Cattle were allowed to graze on special downs, or on newly reclaimed grasslands, but remained beasts of lowland meadows and up until the latter half of the seventeenth century sheep reigned supreme. Occasionally new crops such as Dwarf Rape, Turnips, Red Clover and Lucerne were planted, but these usually failed to do well and frequently failed altogether. Ploughing turned the downs into barren wastelands and the habit of warrening large numbers of rabbits here similarly reduced their potential. All sorts of techniques were employed to try and improve the soil. 'Burn-backing', where the turf was stripped off, piled into heaps and burned, gave disappointing if not disastrous results. Another technique, 'raftering', in which alternate strips of turf were lifted and inverted on to the strips left in place, provided a double sod into which the corn was then sown. Fields subjected to this type of process

LEFT **The downland palette**
RIGHT **Common Field Grasshopper**

Pasque Flower

could only yield two crops before they were exhausted. Finally, in the late 1800s a run of bad seasons ushered in a farming depression which lasted until the end of the First World War. Then in the 1930s a concerted national effort to reclaim downland was initiated. Scrub was grubbed out and the land ploughed and sown with productive commercial leys of Perennial Rye Grass, Cocksfoot and Meadow Fescue. By the late 1940s an increasing battery of chemical and mechanical aids were available, and at last arable farming became economically viable on vast acreages of otherwise useless downland. From then on the scrub was cleared, the hedges torn out, the sheep sheared and led off to market, and the downland destroyed. Only that on steeply undulating slopes, where mechanised operations are impossible, or on a few fragments of military land, have survived the ravages of the last forty years. Downland has even had to endure the scourge of modern forestry and vast tracts of Hampshire's, Sussex's, Dorset's and Wiltshire's chalk grassland are now buried in a tedious spread of woodland planted by the Forestry Commission from the mid-1920s onwards.

As usual the story is a sad one. Like our valuable heathland the remaining British downlands have an international importance. Yet they have been excessively fragmented and maltreated by the armouries of insecticides, herbicides and fungicides. Being spread over the affluent south they now endure more public access as leisure time increases. Whether it is the casual kite-flying picnickers or the careful probing naturalists, the pressure has greatly increased. Trampling, erosion, litter and fire damage are all on the increase and the precious little patches of downland continue to decay. Excessive boot or backside bashing of the turf soon denudes the invertebrate fauna and, if persistent, the botanical richness is reduced, the soil compacted and the site is effectively worn out. Another major problem is the interference with proper grazing. Sheep are kept away from focus points by continuous public activity and here coarse

It's all down to the sheep

grasses soon dominate and eventually form the precursor of scrub. Even when a site is saved from the greater evils of forestry, agricultural, industrial or residential development it remains tortured by the excesses of the 20th century – an age where this habitat is truly alien.

Paradoxically modern downland conservationists need to be farmers to retain this environment. Thus, special flocks of sheep are carefully shepherded over the reserve to maintain a level of grazing which controls scrub invasion and supports the characteristic high species diversity of the flora and fauna. Cattle, ponies, donkeys and goats have all served our interest and where these are beaten by unruly terrain, artificial mowing is employed. Scrub clearance gives blisters to small posses of volunteers, who claw back downland from under Hawthorns and each year a limited number of individuals devote summers to protecting species such as rare birds or orchids. These testimonials highlight an increasingly healthy attitude to realistic ecology, no doubt influenced by the bevy

of educational natural history television programmes and the quality and range of current natural history books. The young are imbued with a firm conservation ethic throughout their schooling and as a result of these inputs, access by nature trails, forest and country parks is still increasing. But, we are still losing.

Until there is a centralised power which generates and maintains a positive strategy for countryside management, which functions as an equal to the forestry, agricultural and industrial needs of the age the future of our downland, or indeed any habitat, will remain threatened. To those with the plough, money makes the down go round, not the trill of the lark, the colour of the orchid, or the smell of a square mile of grass which has turned gold in the glow of every sunset since Agincourt. The light of ecological enlightenment may be burning at its all time brightest, but if I were you I would rub my senses over a few downlands and their inhabitants before it is all too late.

Identification of what is around you will greatly increase your enjoyment of Natural History. The following pages describe the species that are most likely to be encountered in a Grassland habitat. Each species is also featured in a colour plate, representative of the type of habitat in which it is most likely to be found. The combination of the picture and description should enable you to find out what is flying, standing, buzzing or growing in front of you. Unless otherwise stated all the measurements given are, in the case of plants, heights or, in the case of animals, lengths.

Grassland and Scrubland Residents – A GUIDE

LEFT **Cowslips**

SPRING

GRASSLAND RESIDENTS – A GUIDE

SUMMER

ORCHIDS

SUMMER

NIGHT

PLANTS

Wild Mignonette *Reseda lutea* 15–30 cm
This pale green floppy biennial differs from the sweetly fragrant Garden Mignonette, which has orange anthers, in its greenish-yellow flowers, yellow anthers and its pinnate wavy-edged leaves. It is almost confined to chalk and limestone but is absent from most of the north and west, showing a southern and eastern bias in Britain. It normally grows on disturbed ground, path-sides, field edges, verges and bare patches in downland turf, such as those found around rabbit scrapings. Flowers appear from mid to late summer and Mignonette is often locally common, forming a dense faintly fragrant sward.

Common Rock-rose

Helianthemum nummularium Prostrate
This species grows throughout most of the British Isles but is absent from both the south west and north west. It is frequently found on short, grazed chalk grassland, particularly on slopes where loose soil forms open patches. Its yellow flowers appear between May and September and are up to 2.5 cm across. Rock-rose is a shrubby perennial with low, lanceolate, single veined leaves that are green above and downy white beneath. It is also frequently found in garden rockeries.

Meadow Cranesbill

Geranium pratense 30–60 cm
This pretty, hairy perennial has bright blue flowers, slightly tinged with violet, which grow to over 2 cm across and are held on long stalks. Its stem is hairy, often sticky, and reddish coloured. It supports long, deeply lobed stalk leaves. The flowers, which have un-notched petals, appear from June to September and the species is widespread throughout most of Britain, being only absent from northern Scotland and south western England. It is most frequently encountered on roadsides, hedgebanks and in meadows and permanent pastures on chalky soils.

Common Buckthorn

Rhamnus cathartica 2–5 m
This deciduous and thorny shrub has pointed, oval, finely toothed leaves, which enable it to be immediately distinguished from Hawthorn. These leaves are hairless and held on widely spreading branches. Buckthorn flowers in May or June when it gives rise to dense unstalked clusters of small four-petalled green flowers, male and female flowers being borne on different plants. The berries are black and the species is widespread over the British Isles, with the exception of Northern Ireland where it is localised in distribution. Elsewhere it is especially predominant on chalk and limestone grasslands where it sometimes forms dense patches of scrub.

Common Birds-foot Trefoil

Lotus corniculatus Prostrate
This hairless perennial is one of our commonest and brightest yellow pea flowers. It has unstalked, apparently trifoliate leaves, with a lower pair of small oval leaflets, which appear like stipules. The flowers, which appear from late May through to September, are held on a long stalk, with up to eight flowers in a head, each having three sepal-like bracts, often veined or washed with reddish-orange. The seed pods produced are about 3 cm long and are held in a head which resembles a bird's foot and gives the species its name. It is commonly found on the short turf of chalk and limestone grassland, cliff-tops, heath grassland, roadsides, meadows and pasture in well drained places. Like Sainfoin it was formerly used as a forage crop and it can be found over the whole of the British Isles.

Sainfoin *Onobrychis viciifolia* 30–40 cm
This species, with its conspicuous spikes of bright pink flowers, is a downy perennial which appears from June onwards. In the past it was widely grown as a fodder crop, and in many places it appears as a relict of cultivation. It has narrow leaflets held on pinnate leaves and oval seed pods which

are worted, heavily necked, veined and do not burst. Its English name stems from the French and literally means 'wholesome hay'. The species is a strict calcicole, being limited to permanent chalk and limestone grassland on the north and south downs of Hampshire, Wiltshire, Dorset, the Chilterns and East Anglia north to Yorkshire.

Tufted Vetch
Vicia cracca Prostrate and climbing
This slightly downy perennial produces flowers from June through to August. They are held on long, stalked, one-sided spikes and are bright blue-violet, often lending considerable colour to a patch of greenery. The leaves have 8 to 12 pairs of leaflets and terminate in a tendril, each having narrow untoothed stipules at their base. It is a common species of rough grassland, old pastures, roadsides, hedgerows and scrub and is generally distributed over the whole of the British Isles, with the exception of the Scottish uplands.

Silverweed
Potentilla anserina Prostrate
An unmistakable species; this is the only common yellow flower which has silvery pinnate leaves. It is a silky prostrate perennial, has red creeping stems and well toothed leaflets which are alternately large and small. These are silvery on both sides. Silverweed is a familiar plant of roadsides, farm tracks, field gateways, waste ground, disturbed pastures and old arable fields. It is tolerant of trampling and soil compaction and can also be found on sand-dune soil. The largish solitary flowers appear from June to August and are pollinated by various insects. The species is widespread over all of the British Isles, except for parts of northern Scotland.

Salad Burnet
Sanguisorba minor 80 cm
This species is widespread throughout England and parts of Wales but diminishes in abundance north towards Scotland, where it is absent from the Isles. It has a pronounced affinity for chalky soils and limestone grasslands. Its male and female

(hermaphrodite) flowers are held on the same inflorescence which appears between May and August. It is perennial, hairy below and smells of cucumber when crushed. Its leaves are pinnate with small well-toothed leaflets and its tiny flowers are green and held in globular heads which are coloured by the yellow stamens and dark red styles. Its fruits are small four-sided structures with straight ridges.

Hawthorn
Crataegus monogyna 6 m
This common, thick-set and often painfully thorny deciduous shrub has three to five deeply lobed leaves. It flowers in May and June when areas of scrub composed of this species enjoy a brief period of mad cloudy whiteness. Closer observation reveals that the flowers are tinged pink and held on downy stalks in broad umbel-like clusters. They are strong scented and give rise to roundish dull red berries called 'haws'. The species is widespread and abundant all over Britain where it sometimes grows as an understorey in woodland and is frequently used for hedges.

Cowslip
Primula veris 6–18 cm
This famed and familiar downy perennial is easily distinguished by its deep yellow and fragrant flowers which are held in umbels which droop to one side of the leafless stalk. The height of these varies depending on the soil quality, but the 'primrose-like' leaves and pale green inflated calyx are always present. It flowers in April and May in old meadow pastures, grasslands, hedgebanks, open scrub and woodland clearings, and shows a preference for calcareous base-rich soils. It is widely distributed throughout the British Isles, although it is absent from parts of Ireland, Shetland and the Outer Hebrides.

Common Centaury
Centaurium erythraea 4–30 cm
This highly variable hairless annual is sometimes found growing in a cushion of pointed oval prominently-veined leaves. These sprout stems which hold pink flow-

ers in terminal clusters on short branches. The stamens are joined to the top of the corolla tube and the calyx, with its five narrow keeled teeth, is shorter than this tube or the fruit. The species is widespread and locally common on dry grasslands and dunes. It flowers from June onwards. In Scotland it is almost wholly coastal.

Autumn Gentian
Gentianella amarella 4–20 cm
This species, also known as Felwort, is a low, hairless, often purplish, biennial Gentian which has lanceolate leaves. The flowers appear late, in August or September, and usually occur in spikes of five. These are dull purple, and have a neat bell-shaped corolla tube which has a fringe of hairs inside. The species is widespread, occurring most frequently on well-drained calcareous grassland and in dune slacks. There are four sub-species in Britain.

Yellow Rattle *Rhinanthus minor* 6–35 cm
This species is a hairless annual that can be found on permanent pastures, meadows, chalk and limestone grassland, where it is a partial parasite on the roots of other plants, especially the grasses. Between May and August the canary yellow, or syrup coloured, flowers appear in loose spikes. These are individually narrow, two-lipped and somewhat open mouthed, having a straight corolla tube and two, often violet, teeth. The seeds produced later are flat, winged and produce a rattling sound when ripe in the pods. However, the species is very variable, both in time of germination and flowering, and in habitat requirement, and there are numerous sub-species separated by their flowering times and habitat preferences. It is found all over the British Isles.

Elder *Sambucus nigra* 4 m
This small deciduous tree is our only native shrub having opposite pinnate leaves. However, its bark is easily its most conspicuous identification feature. This is deeply fissured and corky, filled with a white pith, and when young the twigs have numerous scales. Its leaves are large and dark green and usually have five lanceolate toothed leaflets with no stipules at their base. Flowers appear in June and July amd are held in large flat-topped umbel-like clusters and are small, fragrant and creamy white in colour. These give rise to a juicy berry which ripens to black from pale green. Elder is common in woods, hedgerows and scrubland, especially on chalk.

Eyebright *Euphrasia officinalis* 2–28 cm
There are a variety of micro-species of Eyebright which are all difficult to separate. They are annuals and partial parasites on the roots of various grassland herbs. Most flower during the late summer, but some appear as early as May and there is a degree of hybridisation between the species. The Common Eyebright is a low, dark and bronzy-green annual with small stiff deeply-toothed oval leaves. Its flowers appear on leafy spikes and have two lips, the lower lip having three spreading lobes which are usually white, but may be tinged with violet or red. These have purple veins and a yellow spot and the species is very variable in size. The whole range of micro-species are widespread in grassy places throughout the British Isles.

Knapweed Broomrape
Orobanche elatior 30–60 cm
This species is more or less confined to lowland southern England where its local distribution is weighted towards Hertfordshire, Cambridgeshire, Dorset and Wiltshire. As its name suggests it is a major parasite of the Greater Knapweed *Centaurea scabiosa* and it thus can be found in rough grassland on the shallow dry chalky soils where this species occurs. It flowers during June and July when its stout honey brown, rigid stem bears the peculiar swollen and bract covered hooded flowers.

Wild Thyme *Thymus praecox* Prostrate
This mat-forming, aromatic perennial has

an extensive creeping root system of runners, which give rise to short flowering stems between June and August. Its leaves are opposite, very small and short-stalked. They are leathery, more or less oval and vary from being almost hairless to quite woolly. Its flowers are reddish-purple and are held in small roundish terminal heads with a dark calyx. Thyme is spread over the whole of the British Isles but is infrequent in the Midlands and East Anglia. Elsewhere it is a common plant of close grazed permanent grasslands, cliff-tops and mature sand dunes. In the south east it is almost entirely confined to the chalk where it is more frequently discovered growing on ant hills.

Devilsbit Scabious
Succisa pratensis 30–90 cm
This hairy perennial has a very short rootstock believed to have been bitten off by the devil. More realistically, it has stalked elliptical leaves which are often blotched with purple. The stem leaves are fewer, narrower and sometimes toothed. Scabious flowers are held in round heads, appear from June onwards, and are dark bluish purple or pink. The plant is ubiquitous throughout the whole of Britain where it grows in wet meadows, marshes, on heathlands, in damp open woods and on mildly acid to calcareous soils. It also occurs frequently on chalk grassland, where it is pollinated by a range of bees and butterflies.

Ox-eye Daisy
Leucanthemum vulgare 30–60 cm
Also known as the Moon Dog or Marguerite Daisy, this species is distributed all over the British Isles but becomes less frequent in Scotland. It is a common plant of grasslands, roadsides, hedgebanks and cliff-tops, usually on chalky or calcareous soils. It is a large perennial daisy, slightly hairy, with small, dark, glossy green well-toothed leaves, the upper being narrow lanceolate and slightly clasping, whilst the lower remain long stalked and spoon

Hogweed

shaped. The flowerheads are solitary and up to 6 cm across with bright yellow disc florets and conspicuous white rays. These appear from May onwards and often cloak whole verges, roads, and scrubby areas in a confetti of white.

Carline Thistle *Carlina vulgaris* 8–30 cm
This stiff spiny biennial has prickly thistle-like leaves, the lower of which are often cottony. It has terminal flowerheads up to 3 cm across usually held in clusters of two to five. These are yellowy-brown, unrayed, with spiny, cottony leaf-like outer bracts and conspicuous purple-based narrow straw-yellow inner bracts which fold over in wet weather. When the flowers die their yellowish remains look much the same as their living counterparts and these relicts often survive the winter. It is a characteristic plant of dry, grazed chalky grasslands and sand dunes and it flowers from July to October when it is pollinated by bees and hoverflies. Carline Thistle is widely distributed throughout England and Wales, but becomes mainly coastal in Scotland.

Common Knapweed
Centaurea nigra 12-70 cm

This downy perennial is also known as 'Hard head' because of its hard based flowerheads which appear from June onwards. These develop from tough globular buds into solitary purple flowerheads with numerous overlapping flat sepal-like bracts, their top part being dark brown or blackish and feathered into fine teeth. It fruits and frequently hybridises with other knapweeds. Its stem is stiff, ribbed and often swollen under the flowerhead. It has lanceolate leaves of which only the lower are toothed. The flowers can be found in grassy places all over the British Isles but it shows a preference for rough grassland and roadsides on heavy or wet soils.

Autumn Lady's Tresses
Spiranthes spiralis 18 cm

This orchid is fairly common on chalk downlands near the sea but can also be found on grassy lawns, tennis courts and even car park frontages. Its inflorescences resemble greeny-white plaits arranged in a tight spiral and each flower is shaped like a bell. Its broad lip resembles a scoop, it has two nectar bands at its base and leaf-shaped pollenia. The stalk is glandular fitted with a basal rosette of withered leaves and beside it the start of a new green rosette which appears in late autumn and winter. Ploughing of many grasslands has reduced its numbers yet it is still widespread in England, Wales and Ireland, but absent from Scotland.

Musk Orchid
Herminium monorchis 8-15 cm

This species can be remarkably inconspicuous in the sward of chalky grassland, but with a keen eye groups of these lily-like plants can be found. The flowers are bell-like, protrude angularly from the dense spike, are yellowish-green and have a short spurred lip like a broad arrowhead. Its leaves are broad, blunt and are held in a group of two or three at the base of the stem. Its distribution is scattered south of a line between the Cotswolds and Kent, and it flowers in June and July.

Fragrant Orchid
Gymnadenia conopsea 30 cm

This species can be easily distinguished from all our other pinkish orchids except the Pyramidal by its long slender nectar spur. It has long leaves which are narrow and strongly keeled, unspotted and held in two ranks up the stem. It flowers in a long dense spike and has a rather rancid sweet fragrance which is strongest early in the evening. The flowers are usually pale purplish-pink and fitted with a short more or less equally three-lobed lip. It favours chalk or limestone grassland, flowers in June and July and is widely distributed over the whole of the British Isles.

Frog Orchid *Coeloglossum viride* 12 cm

This orchid prefers chalky soils, but can also be found in deciduous and coniferous woods and on grassy banks. It is easily overlooked because it has no bright colours to contrast with the surrounding vegetation and at a first glance seems quite unimportant. Frog Orchids have two large blunt-ended elliptical leaves at their base and higher up the stem some narrow pointed leaves. Flowers are greeny-yellow and are irregularly twisted around some supporting leaves. Each has a long, extended, hanging and blunt three-pointed lip and sepals and petals which form a cap which is green, tinged with pink. Its nectar spur is short and flower spikes appear throughout the summer. Widely distributed, it has been found in almost every British county, although it is commonest in the north and west.

Bee Orchid *Ophrys apifera* 15-30 cm

This is the most common of our three or four *Ophrys* species and has a beautifully marked flower which bears a remarkable resemblance to the rear of a small bumble bee. These flowers have bright pink sepals, narrow square-tipped green petals and a brown furry lip which has a pale U marking surrounding a honey-coloured patch. Bee Orchids have a number of very wide greyish-green leaves at the base of the stalk which overwinter. Bee Orchids are found on chalky soils, although roadsides, pastureland and even sandy and gravel tracks can support it. Flowers appear between June and July, often in quite dense clusters in the short turf.

Late Spider Orchid
Ophrys fuciflora 15–25 cm
This beautiful orchid has become much rarer in recent years, because its familiar sites are being disturbed, and it is now limited to a handful of sites along the south coast of England, particularly in eastern Kent. It is an exceptionally variable orchid but the flower often has short broad sepals which are violet-pink to red-purple. The thick hairy brown lip is broadly rectangular, rounded, or even heart-shaped, and has an upright sometimes split point which is usually yellow in colour. The pattern which marks this is more elaborate than on the Early Spider Orchid and consists of a symmetrical three-lobed yellow or pale cream marking filled with stripes and dots of blue and maroon. The stem has a broad rosette of leaves at the base and the plant flowers in early June often on quite steep slopes where there is bare open soil.

Lizard Orchid
Himantoglossum hircinum 30–60 cm
This extraordinary and peculiar orchid is simply so weird that if one were to discover it there is simply nothing else it could be. When in flower the long ribbon-like twisted central lobe on the lip forms a tangled mat lying down the inflorescence. This has a strong goat-like scent which attracts flies, bees and bluebottles. The Lizard Orchid has a few stem leaves which soon wither and a stout spike of short-spurred greyish-green flowers with hooded sepals. The three-lobed lip, which can be up to 5 centimetres long, allegedly resembles a lizard's tail. This plant is an extraordinary sight but despite several population

booms in the past it is now restricted to a handful of sites in southern England where it grows on chalk or limestone grassland and sand dunes. The flowers appear in June and July and are well worthy of a countrywide crossing to see.

Military Orchid *Orchis militaris* 20–40 cm
This very rare species is known only from two or three sites in England. It has a tall powerful stalk and a number of broad thick bright-green unspotted leaves. The multi-flowered broad oval inflorescence looks dull until the flowers open out to a brilliantly contrasting purple and white show. The perianth is folded and cup shaped and resembles a knight's helmet (with an open visor!), and the lip resembles a body with outstretched limbs. The central lobe is marked with neat reddish-purple hairs and the short spur is bent. It favours chalky soils in damp meadows, but it is unlikely that you will find any of these plants, and if you are looking at one it is because you have made a special trip.

Monkey Orchid *Orchis simia* 15–25 cm
Like the Military Orchid if you are fortunate enough to be looking at this species then there is no mistaking it, since you would have made a special visit to one of the two or three sites where this species now remains in Britain. It has acquired its name because its flowers look like tiny spider monkeys. The monkey's body is made up of the lower lip, two narrow lobes at its base form the legs and two outstretched arms emerge from the top of the 'torso', whilst a short central lobe forms the tail. All the lobes are white at the base and are rich violet-red at the extremities and the monkey's head is formed by the perianth. An unusual feature of this orchid is that the lower flowers open first. Flowering occurs in June and is over in a very short period. In Europe it can grow up to 50 centimetres in height.

Burnt Orchid *Orchis ustulata* 15 cm
This species is very localised in south east

England, where variable numbers appear from year to year on the short turf of chalk or limestone downland. Its inflorescence is a compact cylindrical spike with a rounded top, the perianth forms a helmet which is bright red or reddish-violet with the lower flowers becoming pale. These flowers appear at the beginning of June and are strongly scented. They are held on a slender stalk at the bottom of which there are normally three broad short leaves. This species is easy to identify due to its darkened 'burnt' tip of unopened flowers, but will require a special visit to one of the reserves where it still flowers. It is one of our rarest species.

Green-winged Orchid

Orchis morio 10–20 cm

This species was very common over large areas of southern and central Europe, including England, but today it has disappeared in many areas due to improved pastures and accelerated agricultural development. It is a short plant which has a stout stalk surrounded by a number of sheath-like leaves. At its base there are several oblong grey-green leaves forming a rosette. Its inflorescence is widely spaced and looks as if it has been cut off at the top. The purplish-red petals and sepals form a helmet over the saddle-shaped lip which has a dark spotted centre. It grows over most of the British Isles although not in Scotland, flowers in May and June, and is most easily identified by its characteristic flower spike.

Common Spotted Orchid

Dactylorhiza fuchsii 30–50 cm

Probably our commonest orchid this species can be found on calcareous and clayey soils in marshes, meadows, pastures, wasteland, downland, and even on roadside verges. The flowers are very variable in colour but are more robust than its close relative the Heath Spotted Orchid. Its leaves are broad, long and thick. The flowers are held in a pointed spike, their lips are wavy edged, they are marked with crimson

lines and have three well-separated lobes. It too forms frequent hybrids, particularly with the Heath Spotted Orchid, and its flowers are generally of a pinkish hue. It is widespread over the whole of Britain, but is commonest in the south and east.

Early Marsh Orchid

Dactylorhiza incarnata 30–50 cm

The name Early Marsh Orchid provides a collective name for a large number of shapes, varieties, hybrids and ecological groups which are massed under this one species. Other such forms include the White or Fen Early Marsh Orchid, the Bloody Early Marsh Orchid, the Southern Marsh Orchid, the Broad-leaved Marsh Orchid, the Northern Marsh Orchid, and the Narrow-leaved Marsh Orchid. Some are species, many sub-species and the whole lot a confusing array of hybrids which are impossible to separate without the help of a computer to analyse tiny parameters of the shape and form of each individual orchid. However this group is characterised by erect mainly unmarked leaves which have a markedly hooded apex, a robust, straight and somewhat hollow stalk and a cylindrical inflorescence punctuated with prominent bracts. The flowers range from white through to a rich reddish-violet and are waxy in texture. They have a lip which has double loops and a small central tooth which appear very narrow. Since the sides are folded straight back. The nectar spurs are straight. This array of species can be found in marshy fields, overgrown grasslands, woodland clearings, fens and wastelands countrywide and for more accurate identification a book devoted to this sole aim should be sought out.

Man Orchid

Aceras anthropophorum 20–60 cm

This is the only orchid which has a man-like lip (two arms and two legs) which is yellow or brown in colour. The stem is usually about 30 centimetres high and has a few small leaves, the rest being clustered at the base and unspotted. The flowers are held in a rather long narrow spike, have an overall yellow-green or brownish-red colour and are unspurred. The upper perianth forms a hood or 'head' which gives the whole flower its human appearance. The flowers have a faint somewhat nasty smell, which resembles freshly cut grass. Man Orchids prefer limey and chalky soils and are usually found in open scrubland, wooded fields as well as grassy banks and quarries. It is a persistent species which can tolerate a level of public tramping, but it has decreased over much of its range in recent years due to agricultural improvement or building. It is limited to southern England, being locally abundant in Kent and Surrey.

Pyramidal Orchid
Anacamptis pyramidalis 20–30 cm

This species has a few narrow unspotted leaves laced up the stem and a dense pyramidal or dome shaped flower spike. The deep reddish-pink flowers are often 'foxy' smelling. Their dorsal sepal and two petals form a hood above the broad tri-lobed lip and the flower is designed to be pollinated by butterflies. Pyramidal Orchids flower between July and August, are widespread and locally frequent on dry chalk or limestone pastures and are most common throughout the south of England.

You may find it somewhat surprising that this field guide to key species on the British grassland and scrubland is devoid of any precise description of the grasses themselves. This is for several reasons. Firstly, grasses can be very difficult to identify without microscopic examination of some of their floral or leaf structures. Secondly, they are not favoured by amateur botanists for investigation; indeed when faced with a Lizard Orchid or a tuft of Perennial Rye Grass it would take a real grass fiend to focus on the latter. For this reason there follows only a brief outline of the five most familiar species which you will undoubtedly spend most of your time treading on to see the more colourful flowers which inhabit this type of habitat. If, however, you are tempted to identify the grasses, a more precise field guide will be required.

Sheep's Fescue *Festuca ovina* 8–30 cm
This is a very common and variable hairless perennial. It is very tufted with short, very narrow, inrolled, even hair-like, waxy green leaves and this waxiness can make dense swards of this grass precariously slippery. The flowers are held on branched heads which appear in May and July. It is very common on dry chalk grassland.

Perennial Rye Grass
Lolium perenne 50 cm
Perennial Rye Grass is another common variable and hairless perennial which has wiry stems. Its leaves are narrow, shiny and folded when young, and its flowerheads are unbranched, spike-like flat structures which hold many flowers. It is widespread and common in grassy places and is often cultivated for grazing. It flowers between June and August.

Quaking Grass *Briza media* 40 cm
Quaking Grass is a distinctive grass which has glossy, oval, short and triangular purplish flower spikelets which hang on long slender stalks and shake gently in the wind. These pods make the species characteristic and are held on a loosely tufted perennial plant which is common and widespread on most downlands or other dry grasslands. The flowers appear in June and August.

Timothy *Phleum pratense* 1.2 m
This is a stout hairless perennial which has broad and roughish textured leaves. Its flowerheads are unbranched and narrowly cylindrical, growing as much as 15 centimetres long. These structures differ from the next species in that they are rough to the touch. This grass is widespread and common in grassy places and like the former is often cultivated in single species swards for animal foodstuffs.

Pyramidal Orchid

Meadow Foxtail
Alopecurus pratensis 1.2 m
This species is a hairless and tufted perennial. It has roughish leaves but shorter flowerheads which generally only reach 6 to 8 centimetres in length and which are greyish or purplish in colour. They are smooth and silky to the touch. It is widespread in Britain and usually abundant in meadows and on roadsides where it flowers between April and July.

Our grassland habitats are incredibly herb-rich and there are many species which will frequently be encountered on any summer jaunt which have not been outlined above. Tormentil *Potentilla erecta*, Harebell *Campanula rotundifolia*, the Milkworts and the Toadflaxes, Woolly Thistle *Cirsium eriophorum*, Ploughman's Spikenard *Inula conyza*, and Agrimony *Agrimonia eupatoria* are all common species with broad distributions. Yew *Taxus baccata*, Box *Buxus sempervirens* and Wayfaring Tree *Viburnum lantana* join

a host of other species in forming the scrubby areas, and on any botanical foray to grass or scrubland, if the intention is to name the species that you find, then take along one of the excellent modern field guides to aid your exploration.

INVERTEBRATES

Pisaura mirabilis 1–1.5 cm
This is a large, long legged spider with two pairs of fore-limbs held closely together. Its carapace is marked with a broad median band bisected by a thin white or yellow line which ends in a tuft of hairs between the eyes. The spider also has conspicuous 'tear marks' beneath the eyes and a pale abdomen with an irregular outline. The overall coloration varies from grey to olive brown. The species appears in early summer and is common in grassland habitats. In June and July the female's pale egg sac makes her more obvious.

Common Field Grasshopper
Chorthippus brunneus 1.7–2.2 cm
The underside of this medium to fairly large grasshopper's thorax is profusely hairy. Colour variation is so extensive and continuous that it is impossible to make definite distinctions between the hundreds of different morphs. The most common colour varieties are striped or mottled with a mixture of green, pink and olive. Jet black forms can also be found. Adults appear in late June and July, often abundantly in dry areas with open stony areas. The species is a strong flyer and may be very difficult to catch in summer sunshine as it zig-zags madly across its habitat. The song of the male is composed of short brisk chirps, each lasting less than half a second. This species can be found in all parts of the British Isles, excluding the Scottish Uplands and Isles and parts of Northern Ireland.

Meadow Grasshopper
Chorthippus parallelus 1.6–2 cm
This species can be found in all types of

grasslands, wasteland, heathland, or even inland marshes. It has a long season – adults which appear in July can last until early November, being abundant in places. It is incapable of flight and easy to capture, but its song is undeveloped, composed of a burst of stridulation lasting up to three seconds, repeated at irregular intervals. In appearance the Meadow Grasshopper is medium-sized and both sexes have vestigial hind-wings. There are six principle colour varieties, all of which have green on the head and front segment of the thorax. Others are marked with a mixture of brown, pink and red. It is found all over England, Scotland and Wales, but is absent from the Scottish Islands, the Isle of Man and Ireland.

Common Green Grasshopper
Omocestus biridulus 1.6 cm
This species can be found on a great variety of grassland, especially where the vegetation is lush. Woodland clearings, grassy roadsides and paths are also favoured and the species occurs in two morphs, one green and one olive brown. There is no reddish colour on the abdomen and females, which always have a greenish hue, are marked with brown or purple on their sides. Appearing in May the adults are abundant by July when males produce a prolonged ticking song which ends abruptly. It can be found in every corner of the British Isles.

Great Green Bush-cricket
Tettigonia viridissima 4.5 cm
This insect is generally green coloured with a brown, sometimes almost black, stripe along the head and back. It has very well developed wings which usually exceed 7 centimetres in their span and the female's ovipositor is at least 2 centimetres long and slightly downcurved. It is generally found in shrubby areas along hedgerows or in places where its favoured plants, such as thistles, nettles, brambles, bracken, gorse, or very long grass grow. Males frequently stridulate from trees,

often quite high up, and the song, with the exception of that of the Field Cricket, has to be the loudest of any British Orthopteran. It is a harsh high-pitched song which consists of long bursts punctuated by momentary hesitations of varying intervals, usually of between 3 and 20 seconds. When catching or handling these insects care should be taken since they will bite, and the best method of handling is to grip both back legs firmly. Further, if they are kept in captivity they should be kept separate, since cannibalism will result if more than one insect is placed in the same container. This cricket is a southern species and has been recorded in every county south of The Wash, although it is most common along the south coast.

Field Cricket *Gryllus campestris* 2 cm
This species is very rare in Britain being confined to well drained grassland and heath in South Hampshire, West Sussex and Surrey. It is a large cricket, shiny and black in colour with pale yellow markings at the base of its fore-wings. Its hind-wings have been reduced to vestigial stubs, making flight impossible. Large and slow moving, it is one of the earliest Orthopterans to appear, becoming active in its burrow during March. Its song can be heard from a hundred yards or more and they sing throughout the day, beginning in May. The species fares best overall in warm humid conditions with little or no sunshine. In Europe it is more common and in western, central and southern Europe this species is often sold as a pet to children who keep them in open topped jars.

Gatekeeper *Pyronia tithonus* 3.5–4.5 cm
Male Gatekeepers have rich golden brown wings broadly edged with dusky brown and a wide brown streak, carrying scent scales, extending from the front edge to near the centre of the fore-wing. Near the tip of this is a white-centred double eyespot. The hind-wings too are surrounded by a wide dark band leaving a central area of golden brown. Females are

generally lighter in colour. The Gatekeeper is a familiar hedgerow butterfly which can be frequently found feeding on bramble blossoms. It has a weak fluttery flight often seeming to go round in circles and returning to the same sprig of flowers or favourite leaf. It generally rests with its wings closed, but the broad bands of brown which encircle the upper-wing markings are very characteristic and easy to see. The adults are on the wing from late July through to the early part of September the species is common throughout much of England, especially in the south and south west.

Meadow Brown *Maniola jurtina* 5 cm
Male Meadow Browns are dark brown with a small white-centred eyespot near the tip of the fore-wing. Below this there is an area of gingery brown and a patch of dark scent cells. Their hind-wings are similar in colour but are often speckled with darker brown. Females have a larger ginger patch covering most of the outer fore-wing near the tip of which is a large white pupilled black spot. The undersides of both sexes are light brown with a paler wide band and are edged with a wavy brown line which runs across all four wings. Meadow Browns can be almost ridiculously common in some habitats, occurring in sub-plague proportions and feeding on thistles and brambles, their slow floppy flight and apparent loathing to leave their resting place making them easy to observe. They frequent meadows (sic), commons and heaths, hills and downland, and are on the wing from late July until late September, over nearly all of the British Isles.

Dark Green Fritillary
Mesoacidalia aglaja 6 cm
This is our most widely distributed fritillary. It inhabits downs and rough uncultivated pastures, where its powerful wings sweep it effortlessly across the hill-side. These butterflies, which appear in late July and remain on the wing into September, have slightly different sized sexes. Males are a rich golden-brown marked with an intri-

cate pattern of black lines, spots and markings on both fore- and hind-wings. The females are larger and similarly marked but the underside colour and markings of both sexes provide the chief characteristics to separate this species from the other fritillaries. The undersides are marked with green tints filled with olive and gold and the regular pattern of silver discs and spots which forms a chain around the edge of the wing is highly distinctive. Although Dark Green Fritillaries have become rare in many areas they can still be found over much of Britain and in areas scattered all over Ireland.

Duke of Burgundy Fritillary
Hamearis lucina 2.5 cm
Adults of the Duke of Burgundy appear in May on sunny slopes and rough pastures which border woods where they settle on flowers with wings half open. This species is commonest in the southern counties but can be found in the Lake District and Yorkshire although it has much decreased in recent years. Its ground colour is brownish-black and its fore-wings are marked with two irregular transverse bands of orange-brown streaks. The hind-wings are darker, with fewer streaks of the same colour and the margins of these are surrounded by black spots enclosed in orange crescents. Sexes are easily separated at close range because the male only has two pairs of legs, the third pair being vestigial, whilst the female has the normal three pairs in common to all butterflies.

Little Blue *Cupido minimus* 2.2 cm
This butterfly is very local in distribution and is commonest in southern England where it frequents grassy hill-sides, downland and disused chalkpits. It has a rapid fluttering flight which is often low over the ground for short distances and it roosts gregariously on grass stems. The sexes differ; the male is a greyish-black dusted with light silvery-blue scales near the body and the female a dark brown with no suggestion of blue at all. The underside

markings are similar in both sexes, a central black spot and a chain of seven white-ringed black dots running parallel to the wing margin, the hind-wings dotted with twelve scattered black spots. Small Blues emerge at the end of May and live between 10 and 14 days, laying their eggs on the flowers of Kidney Vetch.

Common Blue
Polyommatus icarus 2.8 cm
This is our commonest blue butterfly which is well distributed throughout the British Isles. It frequents hills and meadows, indeed any rough pasture or wasteland, but shows a preference for downland. It has a quick fluttering flight and often alights on grass stems to sun itself with wings half open. There are two broods, the first in late May and throughout June, the second brood appearing in August and September. The sexes are quite distinct, the male being a clear violet blue with white fringes and wings thinly outlined at the margins in black and the female a dull brown, usually marked with a suffusion of violet-blue scaling over both her fore- and hind-wings closest to the body. A chain of orange crescents runs around the margins of all four of her wings which are marked with brown fringes. The underside of the male is pale bluish-grey and the female pale coffee, but the markings are similar in both sexes: a sprinkling of black dots surrounded by white rings, with lines of white and orange and black crescents.

Chalkhill Blue *Lysandra coridon* 3 cm
The sexes of this butterfly are quite distinct. The male is a light silvery blue and has its fore-wing margins outlined in black. Its hind-wings carry a series of six black spots, ringed with white and outlined in black. The female is a dull brown, often dusted with blue scaling near the body. Her hind-wings are marked with a row of black marginal spots, edged with cream and orange crescents. The underside of the male is a pale greyish-blue on the fore-wing with nine white-ringed black spots

edged with a chain of dark markings, whilst its hind-wing carries about a dozen similar spots on a buffish brown colour. The female undersides are similar but are a dark coffee colour, and the markings are usually larger and brighter than in the male. Adults emerge in late July and remain on the wing throughout August and well into September, and are familiar butterflies of chalk and limestone grasslands where their food plant, Horseshoe Vetch, is common. Although their population has decreased in recent years they can still be found in south and south west England and their most northerly outpost is in Lincolnshire. They have a rather manic fluttery flight and often settle with their wings half open to feed on the array of downland flowers.

Adonis Blue *Lysandra bellargus* 2.8 cm
The Adonis Blue butterfly is the most striking of the great British blues. The sexes differ; males being a striking azure blue with the margins of all four wings edged with black and lined with white fringes, females a grey brown occasionally slightly dusted with blue scaling near her body, and marked with a white spot on each fore-wing and a chain of faint orange spots along its margin. Their hind-wings are edged with black spots, ringed with blue, followed by a row of orange crescents edged with black. The underside of the male is grey and the female buff brown and both sexes are sprinkled with small round black spots, each ringed with white. There are two broods, the first emerging at the end of May and the second in late August. They frequent chalk and limestone grassland from Kent to Cornwall, but have declined in recent years. Adonis Blues have a fast fluttering flight which carries them close to the ground and they often pause to feed with wings half open.

Marbled White *Melanargia galathea* 5 cm
The ground colour of this butterfly is creamy white or pale yellow. All four of its wings are marked with irregular black

squares, blotches, and circles which alternate with an equal number of light areas, giving the whole butterfly a piebald appearance. The female is slightly larger and the undersides of both sexes correspond to their upper-sides. They are common on the chalk and limestone downs of southern England, and easily identified by a slow floppy flight low over the grass. They frequently settle on wild flowers to bask in the sun. Adults emerge in the middle of July and remain on the wing for most of August, and Marbled Whites can be found as far north as Yorkshire.

Dingy Skipper *Erynnis tages* 2.5 cm
This skipper is commonest on the chalk downland of southern England although uncultivated pastures, meadows, commons, heaths, banks and hill-sides, as far north as Yorkshire, hold small numbers. It has a fast zig-zagging flight which makes it almost impossible to follow and it basks on bare ground with wings spread wide open. Adults emerge in late April and remain on the wing until mid-June. Both sexes have a ground colour of dull grey-brown, marked with two transverse lines of black spots. These enclose a band of grey and a number of irregular blotches and short lines on the basal half of the wing. The margins are outlined with dark streaks and edged with white spots and the hind-wings faintly sprinkled with white dots and have a pronounced margin of dark spots ringed with white. The undersides are light golden brown with cream coloured spots sprinkled all over.

Grizzled Skipper *Pyrgus malvae* 2.2 cm
The sexes of this butterfly are similar, their ground colour being black, suffused with grey at the base of the wings, all four of which are marked with irregular white spots of varying size. The underside is marbled grey, black dotted, streaked with white and the hind-wings are brownish-grey carrying similar white markings. adults appear in mid-May and remain on the wing through the first part of June,

when their rapid darting flight, often close to the ground, has a similar zig-zagging pattern to that of the Dingy Skipper. Grizzled Skippers frequently bask on bare soil or flowers with wings wide open and are common in southern England on limestone slopes and chalky downlands.

Essex Skipper *Thymelicus lineola* 2.5 cm
This skipper has a fast buzzing flight which usually is only undertaken over short distances. It can often be found feeding on thistle flowers with its hind-wings spread and the fore-wings slightly raised, a position characteristic of this whole family of butterflies. It emerges in late July and flies throughout August across many of the hillsides and downs of south east England. It is absent from Wales, Scotland and Ireland. The sexes are almost identical and have an upper-side colouring of golden brown, with the front edge of the fore-wing and outer margins of both wings edged with narrow bands of black. Essex Skippers can be separated from the Small Skipper by the examination of their antennae which are brown on the upper surface and cream underneath.

Small Skipper *Thymelicus flavus* 2.2 cm
The ground colour of this butterfly is a light golden brown marked with olive brown at the base of the wings. The fore-wings of the male carry a line of blue scent scales from the centre to the hind margin. The underside is a pale creamy yellow with a large wedge of olive yellow covering the front half of the hind-wings. The antennae are black on the upper surface and cream coloured underneath, with orange tips which enable separation from the very similar Essex Skipper. Adult Small Skippers live for 10 to 14 days and emerge in July through to August. They are common over much of England, as far north as Yorkshire, where they can be found on waste ground, meadows and fields, grassy hill-side and limestone downland.

Silver-spotted Skipper

Broomrape

Hesperia comma 3.5 cm
This species has recently declined and is now limited to the chalk downland of southern England, where some isolated populations remain locally common. It has a fast flight, darting from flower to flower, and basks in the sunshine with its wings spread open. It emerges in early August. The males have golden brown fore-wings with a darker band along the margins marked with dull yellow spots near the tip. The hind-wings are brownish-grey spotted with golden brown. The slightly larger females have the base of the fore-wings washed with a golden brown, marked with irregular square yellow spots. The underside of the fore-wing is green at the tip, spotted with cream, and the hind-wings are mustard green, spotted with white.

Large Skipper *Ochlodes venatus* 3.5 cm
This is the largest and most widespread of the British skipper butterflies. It is common over much of England and Wales and only absent from Scotland and Ireland. Found in woodland clearings and ridings, along country lanes, in rough pasture and on downland, it is a very active insect, flitting from flower to flower, often settling on grass stems to bask, in the usual skipper attitude, with the fore-wing raised high over the body. Adults appear in June and remain on the wing until mid-August. The males are fulvous brown with a sloping band of scent cells on the fore-wing and a series of orange-brown spots. The hind-wings are marked with some golden brown spottings, and all four of the wings are edged with black and yellow fringes. Females are slightly larger, have more defined spotting and a darker brown colour. The undersides of both sexes are creamy yellow grading to dull green at the tips and almost black at the base.

Burying Beetle
Nicrophorus vespilloides 1.6 cm
These thick-set, heavily structured beetles are predominantly black, with two striking reddish yellow bands traversing their elytra. In some forms these bands may be reduced to kidney shaped patches. There are several similar species, separated by their various tufts of hair and degrees of blackness, but all of these burying, or sexton beetles can be found around carcasses on grassland. They are carnivorous, feeding on the blowfly larvae which inhabit the corpses which these beetles prepare for their young.

Dor Beetle *Geotrupes stercorarius* 2.6 cm
There are six species of dor beetle of which this may be the most frequently encountered. It is local in distribution and only found as far north as Staffordshire. Their strong but awkward flight often causes them to blunder into you as they travel over their grassland habitat. The elytra is shiny and striated, and all three pairs of legs are fitted with highly developed comb-like structures which aid dung collection. These insects may be fitted with exaggerated horny structures more typical of a tropical beetle. They range in colour

from a bluish or greenish metallic sheen through to a dark black. Many are infested with an ackerine louse which gives rise to their local name of 'Lousy watch-men'.

Soldier Beetle *Rhagonycha fulva* 1.2 cm
This species is only common south of the Midlands, is absent from Scotland and occurs in isolated parts of Ireland. Its legs, thorax and elytra are reddish-yellow. These beetles can often be found in large numbers on flowering umbellifera, where they are very active and enjoy the sunshine. They readily fly, are carnivorous and have soft bodies. Their reddish coloration gives this species the misleading name of 'Blood-sucker' in many parts of the country yet its carnivorous habits are probably directed at other flower visiting species.

Glow-worm *Lampyris noctiluca* 1–1.8 cm
Sexes are clearly distinct; the males, possessing both wings and elytra, are pitch-coloured and covered with a light brown pubescence. The sides of the thorax and the apex of the abdomen are yellow, the elytra is sculptured, and the front of the thorax is extended over the head. This facet is also seen in the female which has no elytra or wings and is laviform in structure. She is brownish with yellowish legs and is fitted with three strongly luminescent structures on her last three abdominal segments. Glow-worms are widespread but local in their habitat, preferring grassy slopes on heaths or open grasslands and they appear throughout the summer.

Attempting to identify all of the insects found in our grass and scrubland habitats would be impossible, even for a whole series of books this size. The great diversity of plants provides food for a huge number of herbivorous insect species and consequently the range of carnivorous forms which feed on these is equally large. I'm afraid there are thousands, creeping and crawling about, for you to find.

The grasshoppers outlined above are commonly joined by Striped-winged *Strenobothrus lineatus* and Rufous Grasshoppers *Gomphocerippus rufus*, both species which can be readily found and identified with a little practice by the amateur naturalist.

Other butterflies include the Wall *Lasiommata megera*, the Brown Argus *Aricia agestis*, and the somewhat isolated Lulworth Skipper *Thymelicus acteon*, which is only to be found in parts of southern England. Migrant butterflies include the Short *Everes argiades* and Long-tailed *Lampides boeticus* Blues, the Queen of Spain Fritillary *Issoria lathonia* and both Clouded *Colias crocea* and Pale Clouded Yellows *Colias hyale*. The latter two species can quite often be seen on south coast grasslands during summer if the conditions are favourable for a Channel crossing. The Small Heath *Coenonympha pamphilus* and Orange Tip *Anthocharis cardamines* butterflies may also be found.

There are of course a great many moth species which thrive on our grassland, as well as a host of Hymenoptera (bees, wasps and ants), all of which would require specialist identification. Indeed the guidelines above have only outlined the more obvious or dramatic species which you are likely to encounter, and if you come across others, use the wealth of good modern field guides to identify them.

VERTEBRATES

Kestrel *Falco tinnunculus* 35 cm
The most common and easily the most conspicuous predator to be seen hunting over our grassland and scrubland, the Kestrel is readily distinguished by its hovering behaviour. In general flight, however, its pointed wings and long narrow tail make it discernible from the more broadly winged and shorter square-tailed Sparrowhawk. Males have a lavender blue-grey tail punctuated by a thick black sub-terminal band, spotted chestnut upper parts, warm buff under parts and grey heads, whilst females have rusty brown and barred upper parts and a

barred chestnut tail. If not hovering, Kestrels perch in a conspicuous place, on the lookout for prey. Flight is with rapid wing-beats, and occasional short glides. Its call is a shrill repeated *Kee, kee, kee, kee*, although the species is usually silent outside the breeding season.

Grey Partridge *Perdix perdix* 30 cm
Red-legged Partridge
Alectoris rufa 35 cm
At a great distance, with very poor binoculars, in a hailstorm these species can be confused. With a half-reasonable view the long white eyestripe, black bordered white gorget on the throat, the lavender flanks (which are heavily barred with chestnut, black and white), the chestnut crown and the conspicuous red bill and legs of the Red-legged Partridge make it easily separable from the generally dingier Grey.

Both are rotund, chicken-like, birds with short rounded wings and a short rufous tail. Flight is low and rapid with alternate spells of whirring wing-beats and gliding on deeply bowed wings. The Grey Partridge has a pale orange chestnut face and a subtle grey neck and breast, the male having a conspicuous dark horseshoe mark on its lower breast, and the bill is a creamy colour. The bird is a fast runner, often giving a grating *Kree-arit* or a rapid *Eck-eck-eck-eck*, whilst the Red-legged Partridge utters an entirely different *Chuck, chuck-er.* In Britain the Red-legged Partridge shows a distinct easterly bias, and is most common in parts of East Anglia and parts of eastern southern England. It is not found in much of Wales, northern England, Scotland or Ireland. This affinity for drier country is not seen in the Grey Partridge which has begun to show a more westerly bias in the British Isles, whereby it is common in the west country, Wales, central southern England, much of the lowlands of Scotland and parts of Ireland.

Barn Owl *Tyto alba* 46 cm
This is the only British owl which appears obviously white, and which hunts almost entirely at night. Its upper parts are pale golden buffish fine specklings, and its under parts minutely speckled with brown dots. It has no ear-tufts, small black eyes and perches upright when its long legs and large head are distinctive. Its voice is very varied, but a long wild shriek or a mixture of hissing, snoring and yapping, can be heard. Unfortunately decreasing through much of its range the Barn Owl is now absent from many areas where it was not uncommon as little as ten years ago. Where it can still be found it is partial to human habitation and frequently breeds in farm buildings, church towers, ruins, water towers, or occasionally on cliffs.

Skylark *Alauda arvensis* 18 cm
One of the commonest and most familiar of all British birds, this mainly brown lark has buffish white under parts and a boldly streaked breast. It is most easily distinguished by its vertical song-flight, often to a great height, where the bird will become indistinguishable as the watcher squints into the hazy sky. From nowhere there will be a high pitched musical outpouring, a trill which can last a matter of minutes. This song may also be delivered from a perch. The most often heard call note delivered in the long shallow undulating flight is a clear liquid *Chir-r-up*. The Skylark's wings are long and have splayed tips with a white trailing edge and the dark tail, again edged with white, is conspicuous in flight. Both the bill and the eyes are small. Between October and March Skylarks can be seen in flocks over arable land.

Nightingale *Luscinia megarhyncha* 16 cm
This shy skulking bird is very difficult to see in the thick vegetation that it inhabits in our woods, copses and shrubby areas. It is only its famous song, which can be heard by day and night, which makes it easy to identify and locate. This is rich, loud, and musical, each note being repeated several times. The most characteristic sequences are a deep bubbling *Chook-chook-chook-chook* and a slovenly *Piu, piu, piu, piu*

which terminates in a shattering crescendo. Making visual contact with Nightingales in Britain requires a degree of patience, although occasionally they may rise from the thicket to the outskirts of a bush and allow you fleeting glimpses of their uniform warm brown upper parts and whitish brown under parts shown off by a characteristic brownish chestnut tail. In Britain they occur locally south of a line between the Severn and Humber and in southern Europe and on migration Nightingales seem much less shy and better views of them can be obtained.

Grasshopper Warbler
Locustella naevia 12 cm

This must be one of Britain's most irritating little brown jobs, because it is easily located by its high pitched distinctive song, yet so infrequently glimpsed, as it jumps about in the bottom of rank grass and thick vegetation. The song is a far-carrying mechanical churring, on one high note, like the continual winding of a fishing reel and may be drawn out for as long as two minutes. At times it is even ventriloquial, presumably an effect given by the bird turning its head. It is delivered day or night, but early morning and early evening seem to be most frequent times of delivery. In vision the bird has a rounded tail and oval wings but its attitude can vary between dumpy and slim. In colour it has olive upper parts with subdued dark and lightly streaked buffish white under parts. It can creep and run with great agility amongst the undergrowth, but always seems reluctant to fly. Although much decreased in numbers in recent years the Grasshopper Warbler enjoys thick undergrowth in marshes, water meadows, dry heaths, hedgerows or shrubland over most of the British Isles, excluding the Scottish Uplands.

Whitethroat *Sylvia communis* 14 cm
Lesser Whitethroat *Sylvia curruca* 13 cm

The Whitethroat is the *Sylvia* warbler which is most commonly seen; it is a lanky, restless and manic little bird which has a long tail and comic face. Its song is a strong desperate scratchy chatter which is given from a bush-top or in a brief dancing song flight, terminating with a dive into a hedge. In coloration is has conspicuous rusty wings and a long tail with white outer feathers, the male having a pale grey cap which extends to its nape and below the eye, and a pure-white throat. Its under parts are pale pinkish buff and in general coloration the female is duller with a brownish head and faint pink on her breast. The Lesser Whitethroat is easily distinguished by its shorter tail, much greyer upper parts, dark ear coverts and lack of chestnut in its wings. This is a restless species which is more skulking than the Whitethroat. Its song is a distinctive rattle, beginning with a subdued warble and terminating in an outburst of a single rattling note. This is delivered from thick cover and not from a song flight, as in the Whitethroat. In flight, although brief from bush to bush, with practice its shorter tail and smaller, greyer appearance make it separable from its cogener. Both species prefer open country studded with bushes, brambles, gorse or nettle beds. Whitethroats occur all over the British Isles whilst Lessers are absent from Ireland, Scotland and parts of central England and Wales.

Garden Warbler *Sylvia borin* 14 cm

The call note of this species is very much like the Blackcap's but slightly less harsh and its song has the same mellow quality but is generally quieter and more sustained (see Blackcap). The Garden Warbler is usually seen flitting from bush to bush, when its shortish tail distinguishes it from the Blackcap. It is a plump and uniformly brownish warbler with paler under parts and a characteristic round head and stubby bill. It can be distinguished from female and juvenile Blackcaps by the lack of a brownish crown and apparently, for those with 'bionic' vision, the legs have a bluish tinge. This is a summer visitor worth getting to grips with since it is neat, compact and always appears well groomed, making it one of the prettiest of our *Sylvia* species. It inhabits woods, thickets, bushy commons and bramble patches, overgrown hedges and even fruit-bushes over most of the British Isles. It is absent from much of Ireland and the north of Scotland.

Blackcap *Sylvia atricapilla* 14 cm

This slim elegant warbler has longish wings and tail and an active and lively attitude. Males are distinguished by their glossy black crown, their greyish brown upper parts, and sides of head and under parts of ashy grey. Females have a red-brown crown and browner under parts, and in the swift jerky flight the tail is conspicuously long. The voice is an emphatic *Tac, tac*, which is repeated rapidly when birds are alarmed, and the song is a remarkably rich warbling which is more varied and less sustained than the Garden Warbler, often being louder towards the end of its delivery That is valueless information to anyone who is not an afficionado of the *Sylvia* warblers. It is, however, well worth pursuing until you distinguish its song, as it is with all of this group of birds, because this will save hours in future poking around and squinting into scrub wondering which species is making that particular whittery rattle.

Willow Warbler

Phylloscopus trochilus 11 cm

This is the most common summer visitor to the northern half of Europe and is readily confused with the Chiffchaff. It is a less arboreal species, which is more fond of low vegetation and scrubby areas where it is readily seen, sitting, hovering, or chasing small flies. They are less dumpy, broader winged and generally look greener above and yellower below than Chiffchaffs. Apparently Willow Warblers have pale brown as opposed to Chiffchaffs' black legs, but of course this is another one of those useless field guide legends! Their song, however, is very char-

acteristically different; the Willow Warbler utters a liquid musical cadenza which begins quietly and becomes clearer and more deliberate until it descends to a flourishing *Sooeet-sooeetoo*. Its call is a two syllable *Hooeet* and this can be heard in every crevice of the British Isles.

Linnet *Carduelis cannabina* 13 cm

This finch has a rapid twittering flight call and a song which is a varied musical twitter interspersed with nasal notes which is usually delivered from the top of a bush. In their bounding and energetic flight Linnets appear long winged and long tailed and have white in their wings and at the base of their tail. Males have chestnut brown mantles, dark brown wings and a greyish head with under parts of buff streaked with blackish brown. In the breeding season the breast is pinkish and the crown bright crimson. Females lack this crimson and are generally more streaked. Linnets can be found in almost all open country with shrubby bushes, ranging from heathland, grassland, farmland to marshes. They are distributed widely over the British Isles where in places they are common.

Yellowhammer *Emberiza citrinella* 16 cm

This bird is one of the most commonly seen species in fields, hedges and scrubland all over the British Isles. It is usually found in pairs, although in winter it forms large feeding flocks with other species, and can be seen in many other marginal habitats. Often heard before it is seen the song is a rapid *Chi-chi-chi-chi-chi . . . chweeee*, which allegedly says 'little-bit-of-bread-and-no-cheese'. This is delivered from the tops of bushes, overhead wires, or even posts. Males have lemon-yellow head and under parts and conspicuous chestnut rump, whilst females and juveniles are much less yellow and have darker markings, particularly on the head. Both sexes continually flick their tail, and in flight are noticeably long winged and long tailed.

Poppy

Cirl Bunting *Emberiza cirlus* 16 cm

Once much more widespread across the scrublands of England, the Cirl Bunting is now very restricted to a few coastal haunts in Devon and Cornwall. The male has yellow under parts with a greenish breastband, a black throat, and an olive green head which is capped with a dark crown and has yellow stripes above and below the eye. This characteristic pattern is unique among buntings, and the species is separated from the Yellowhammer by its more heavily streaked appearance, both on its back and its breast, and by its olive, rather than chestnut, rump. The flight call is a weak *Sip* or *Sissi-Sissi-sip*, whilst the song is a monotonous hurried jingle on one note which is reminiscent of the Lesser Whitethroat, if you know what that is like. Juveniles are easily confused with Yellowhammers, but this species is now best encountered on a holiday in Europe, where it frequents tall hedgerows and trees bordering cultivated land, downs, or bushy or rocky hillsides.

Corn Bunting *Miliaria calandra* 18 cm

This is our largest and grossest looking bunting. It is a heavily-built brownish bird, streaked above and below and with no white on its wings and tail. It can be distinguished from other buntings, larks and pipits by its much larger size, round head and stubby bill which give it overall a rather ugly appearance. It is most readily located by its song, which it delivers whilst sitting conspicuously on wires, fence posts, or other perches, and sounds like tinkling keys punctuated by sharp *Quit* call notes. Another characteristic feature is its heavy flight often with dangling legs. Corn Buntings show a preference for open country, usually arable, and are distributed throughout the British Isles, although in many areas they have become localised in the last few years.

Attempting to name and describe all of the birds that could be found on our grass and shrublands is impossible for this short guide. I have presumed that the reader is familiar with species such as Blackbird *Turdus merula*, Song Thrush *Turdus philomelos*, Great Tit *Parus major*, Wren *Troglodytes troglodytes* and Dunnock *Prunella modularis*, which are as much garden or parkland birds as birds which could be seen in our shrubland habitats. Long-tailed Tits *Aegithalos caudatus* and Goldfinches *Carduelis carduelis* are two more species which can frequently be found.

Cuckoos *Cuculus canorus* are present because they parasitise Dunnocks, Meadow Pipits *Anthus pratensis* and Tree Pipits *Anthus trivialis*, which are frequently inhabitants of this habitat. Two further species are worthy of mention. The Cetti's Warbler *Cettia cetti* is a scrub loving bird, but only if the scrub is adjacent to some wetland which provides the bulk of its diet. This newly colonised warbler has spread rapidly in the seventies and eighties, to be almost common in many places along the south coast of England. Unfortunately, the Turtle Dove *Streptopelia turtur* has shown a decline in the same period, and is now almost restricted to areas of quiet scrubland when once it was a common bird over much of the British Isles. Today it is most easily located by its purring call which can be heard when it arrives from its African wintering haunts in early May.

Mole *Talpa europaea* 16 cm
Moles have short black velvety fur and massive heavily clawed fore-teet, a short tail and minute eyes. This, combined with their tapering snout, makes them an altogether attractive animal. Unfortunately they are rarely seen on the surface of the ground, and only their molehills give a clue to their presence. The larger more permanent mounds, known as fortresses, incorporate in their core a nesting chamber. This is filled with grass in order to house the young Moles which are born in April and May and leave the fortress a month later. Moles mainly feed on earthworms and the larvae of beetles and flies. They can be found in almost any habitat where there is suitable soil, avoiding only that which is extremely shallow, stony, heavily waterlogged or in any way worked by man. They are common and widespread over the whole of the English, Welsh and Scottish mainland, but are absent from Ireland and most of the outlying Scottish Isles.

Common Shrew *Sorex araneus* 11 cm
Pygmy Shrew *Sorex minutus* 9–10 cm
In the field shrews are not easily seen by the exploring naturalist, indeed they are more frequently heard when involved in their noisy territorial fights. These shrill screams may be prolonged for up to 30 seconds and can be heard during summer on the edges of paths and in thick grassland. If seen the species are easily separated; there is a sharp contrast between colour of back and flank in the Common Shrew, which is lacking in the uniformly coloured Pygmy Shrew. In the winter and the second (adult) summer pelage the back of the Common Shrew is dark brown, and it has paler brown flanks and grey yellow-tinged under parts. Its tail is bi-

coloured and well haired, whilst that of the Pygmy Shrew becomes hairless in its second year. This species is a medium brown above and has a dirty white ventral pelage, and is both considerably lighter and smaller than the Common Shrew. Both species can be found in almost every habitat, providing there is low cover, but both are most abundant in thick grass, hedgerows, bushy scrub and under bracken. Their movements are swift and bustling as they manically explore with their mobile snout. Both of these insectivores are widespread in Europe, except for the Mediterranean region. In the British Isles the Pygmy Shrew occurs on all of the mainland, including Ireland, and most of the Scottish offshore islands, whilst the Common Shrew is absent from Ireland, the Isle of Man and some of the Inner and Outer Hebrides.

Rabbit *Oryctolagus cuniculus* 40 cm
If any reader requires a paragraph to identify this species I suggest they take this book to a quiet area of grassland and beat themselves slowly to death with it!

Brown Hare *Lepus capensis* 52–60 cm
These fellows can be distinguished from the Rabbit by their longer black tipped ears, longer legs and loping gait, and generally more etiolated appearance. In some northern areas they can be separated from Mountain Hares by their longer ears, brighter yellowish-brown colour and dark upper surface of their tails. Their colour is generally a warmer brown than the Rabbit, and they are white under their cheeks and inside their legs, and have ruddy yellow feet. The highest densities of hares can be found on plain country, the chalks of southern England and limestones of the eastern counties, where they inhabit agricultural land and rough pasture, where areas of scrub or woodland provide suitable shelter. Hares will often crouch low to the ground, ears flat against their head and allow a close approach. Their trails may be obvious over their grassland habitat and

their tracks are characteristic, large elongated impressions of rear feet side by side and showing five toes when pushed into soft ground. Their droppings are usually paler and more fibrous than those of the Rabbit. In Britain hares are widespread on low ground, but population densities have decreased recently in many areas of marginal habitat.

Bank Vole
Clethrionomys glareolus 9–11 cm
Field Vole *Microtus agrestis* 9–11.5 cm
These two species are readily separated if you are fortunate enough to obtain a clear view of the rodent as it scuttles through its grassland home. The Bank Vole has a coat which is a rich reddish-brown on the upper surface, more prominent ears and a tail which is longer than the Field Vole's, being half of the head to body length. In comparison the Field Vole is a small greyish-brown animal with smaller ears and eyes, whose coat colour may have tints of yellow but never shows the chestnut colour of the Bank Vole. The presence of voles is best detected by a network of well formed runways at ground level amongst the cover. Recent use of these is indicated by the presence of greenish-tinged oval droppings, if they are Field Voles', or generally blacker, if they are Bank Voles'. The Field Vole frequents rough ungrazed grassland including young forestry plantations or any scrubby area where a lush growth of grass is present. Only low density populations can be found in marginal habitat such as woodland, hedgerows, dunes, or scree. Here the Bank Vole is more abundant, and this species generally does not move far into fields, because it shows a definite preference for thicker cover, with a high herb and scrub layer. Both species are abundant and widespread over all of Europe and the British Isles, where they are only absent from a number of offshore islands, including the Isle of Man, and in the case of the Field Vole, from Ireland. A population of Bank Voles can be found in south western Ireland.

Harvest Mouse
Micromys minutus 5–7 cm
This is Britain's smallest rodent, and can be easily distinguished from the other mice by its blunt nose and small hairy ears, reminiscent of a vole. Its sparsely haired tail is the same length as its body and is prehensile. The delicate adults have a rusty russet-orange coat and a white belly, and juveniles have a grey-brown coat, similar to that of House Mice. This species favours areas of tall dense vegetation such as long grass, reed beds, rushes, grassy hedgerows, ditches and bramble patches, but discovering them in the field is an unlikely possibility, and the best guides to their presence are their breeding nests, which can be found up to 60 cm above ground level in vegetation. These neat spherical balls are difficult to find in summer, but in winter can stand out clearly. In Britain the Harvest Mouse is most common south of a line from the Humber to the Bristol Channel, although small populations can be found in Wales, Cheshire and Yorkshire.

Red Fox *Vulpes vulpes* 100–108 cm
This species should not need a detailed description. Its erect black-backed ears, slender nose, and long horizontally held bushy tail, its white muzzle, underside of chin, throat and tail tip, its black socks, and slender dog-like stance are surely familiar to every living naturalist. Discerning the presence of this species is relatively easy field-craft. Definite runs are often used and where these pass through hedges, or rusty fences, or bramble patches there are usually a few tell-tale red hairs adhering to any snags. Footprints too are easily distinguished from those of dogs being more oval in shape, with the two centrally placed pads not overlapping with the two side pads. Fox faeces are usually pointed and may be linked together loosely by hairs; when they are fresh they are usually black and have a characteristic odour, and they may often be placed on prominent objects such as stones, fallen branches,

mole hills, or human artefacts. Sex is difficult to assess in the field, and excellent views are required to note the light coloured fur over the male's scrotum which is about the only reliable separation feature. The most frequent calls are intermittent high pitched barks, usually in phrases of two or four and also a single hoarse wailing bark. Foxes are widely distributed over all of the British Isles and are absent only from some of the Scottish Islands.

Stoat *Mustela erminea* 33–45 cm
Weasel *Mustela nivalis* 19–30 cm
These two typical mustelids are easily distinguished but frequently confused by naturalists. The black tip of the Stoat's tail is distinctive at all times, and the Weasel, which has a relatively shorter tail, is always considerably smaller than the Stoat. Indeed its very small size, slender body and more exaggerated movement make it discernible from all other Mustelidae. The coat colour of both species is variable and ranges from a deep rusty brown to a light sandy tan. The winter pelage of both species in the northern parts of their range (although it is very rare to find a Weasel in northern Britain) is an ermine condition of pure white with a black-tipped tail. Both species show a cosmopolitan choice of habitat and a close correlation to cover and potential food supplies: Weasels being prevalent where there are large numbers of voles and mice. In general they are infrequently seen, but occasionally they can be seen dashing across or along paths, up the sides of hedgerows, stone dykes, fence lines, or other natural corridors which traverse grassland. Their gait is bounding and both use regular hunting routes, and are active by both day and night. Both species are widely distributed over the British Isles, however, the Weasel is absent from Ireland, and a few offshore islands on the Scottish coast.

Roe Deer
Capreolus capreolus
Shoulder height 64–68 cm

This neat small deer appears almost tailless, although females do have a small anal tuft of hair. Its black nose and white chin are also distinctive, and when alarmed the hairs of the rump patch are frequently erected to form a powder-puff, as the deer crashes away through the herbage. Coat colour varies from sandy to bright reddish-brown with paler under parts in summer and from greyish-brown to nearly black with a buff belly in winter. Their presence in an area can be discerned by their footprints and droppings, which are shiny black cylindrical pellets, having one end pointed and the other indented, and usually measure about 1.4 by 0.8 cm. In some isolated areas they may be diurnal, but most Roe Deer are nocturnal. They are solitary for much of the year, although small groups of male, female and young may congregate in winter. Roe also utter a characteristic barking call which ranges from a sharp high pitched cry to a harsh brutal bark. Their antlers are small and rarely exceed 30 cm in length, and each antler is composed of a simple structure of three tines. These are cast from late October to December.

The British fauna is rather starved of mammals compared to that of continental Europe. Other than those described above, only the following may possibly stray into grassy areas or scrubland. If this habitat is adjacent to woodland, then both Wood Mice *Apodemus sylvaticus* and Hedgehogs *Erinaceus europaeus* may be heard if not seen. If there are damp streams or human habitation present then the Common or Brown Rat *Rattus norvegicus* may also be seen scurrying across the path, although this much persecuted rodent is perhaps wisely quite a shy animal. Badgers *Meles meles* will forage out of woodland onto grassland where they turn over dung, dig out bees' nests or dig for worms to supplement their diets, and both Sika *Cervus nippon* and Fallow Deer *Dama dama* will, in some parts of their range, stray from their more afforested habitat haunts.

BRITISH GRASS AND SCRUBLAND NATURE RESERVES

What follows is a county by county list of Nature Reserves which are composed of areas of grassland or scrubland. Whilst it may be useful in that it indicates sites of both local and national importance and outlines the species that can be encountered on a visit, it fails to encompass the many millions of tiny grassy or scrubby fragments which can be found almost anywhere in Britain. These you can find by walking suitable roadpaths or footpaths near your home or, if you are a city dweller, by investigating the patches of urban 'wasteland' that occur in your neighbourhood. Many of these unmarked sites will have a few of the species described in this book. However, for serious investigation of the more specific or rarer species a journey may be necessary and here it is worth mentioning the timing of your visit. Some plants may only flower for a few weeks, so to be sure of a good show check before you go. Speak to someone who has been before, or telephone the warden or local Nature Trust headquarters. Do not rely on book dates as the flowering times of some species, particularly the orchids, may vary from site to site. There is nothing, absolutely nothing, worse than driving halfway across the land to look at a well shrivelled orchid that must have been magnificent a week ago.

ENGLAND

Avon and Somerset

Mendip Conservation Area. FT
482545. 586 ha. Somerset Trust for Nature Conservation (STNC)
This collection of Cheddar limestone reserves is represented by Black Rock, Long Wood, Velvet Bottom and others, which form a beautiful matrix of habitats which includes woodlands, scrub, grasslands and craggy cliffs. The grassland is rich in limestone flowers which include Primrose, Eyebright, Lady's Bedstraw, Common Rock-rose, Common Centaury, Wild Thyme, Common Birds-foot Trefoil, Slender St John's Wort, Quaking Grass, Carline Thistle, Dwarf Thistle, Harebell and Small Scabious. The sides of Velvet Bot-

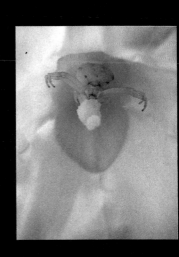

LEFT **Scrub encroachment**
RIGHT *Misumenia vatia*

tom are rich in limestone flora, but the bottom is so contaminated with heavy metals that intensive grazing is dangerous. Thus the grassland here is deep and coarse, providing an excellent site for many of our grassland butterflies. The whole area's interest is further swollen by the archaeological features, such as the Rhino cave in Long Wood, where Pleistocene mammal remains have been found.

Others: Avon Gorge (ST 553731), Breen Down Sanctuary (ST 296586), Brown's Folly (ST 798664), Bubwith Acres (ST 470537), Dolbury Warren (permit only, Avon Wildlife Trust, AWT), Dundon Beacon (permit only, STNC), Goblin Combe (permit only, AWT), Great Breach Wood (permit only, STNC), Ham Hill Country Park (ST 478167), Middle Hope (ST 330660), Rodney Stoke (permit only, NCC), Thurlbear Wood (permit only, STNC)

Bedfordshire and Huntingdonshire

Totternhoe Knolls. SP 986216. 14 ha. Bedfordshire and Huntingdonshire Naturalists' Trust (BHNT) – Bedfordshire County Council

This area has been conspicuously manipulated by man for hundreds of years. The Normans built a castle, and the results of much more recent quarrying are the hills and holes, known as knolls, which are covered with a great range of chalkland plants. Lady's Bedstraw, Common Birds-foot Trefoil, Salad Burnet, Cowslip, Eyebright, Basil and Wild Thyme, Yellow Rattle and Yellow-wort, Wild Mignonette and Quaking Grass are the common conspicuous species. Several orchid species appear in summer, together with Adder's-tongue, Clustered Bellflower, Autumn Gentian and both Horseshoe and Kidney Vetch. At the edge of the woodland, Hawthorn, Sycamore, Bramble and Wild Rose thicken the scrub to provide dense nesting habitat for birds which include most of the grassland specialities. The shorter grassland has many moths and butterflies and some 40 species of Hymenoptera have been recorded. These include several species of those shell-nesting mason bees.

Others: Bankside (permit only, BHNT), Old Warden Tunnel (permit only, BHNT), Pingle Wood Cutting (permit only, BHNT), Upwood Meadows (permit only, BHNT – NCC), Wymington Meadow (permit only, BHNT)

Berkshire

The proportion of grassland to arable in Berkshire today is at its lowest ebb, although 50 years ago the reverse was true. Nevertheless all types of grassland can be found in this county from the acid ridges of Windsor Great Park, with their flora of mosses, ferns and lichens, to the orchid-rich chalk turf of the Berkshire Downs, Inkpen Downs or Winter Hill near Maidenhead. On this chalk there are at least two good colonies of Pasqueflower, a few remaining sites for avian rarities such as the Stone Curlew and lepidopteran specialities such as Adonis Blues and Silver-spotted Skippers. Along the edge of the Thames between Streatley and Reading there are some rich alluvial meadows, at least one of which holds a great number of Snake's-head Fritillaries. All of these sites need individual attention and exploration, whilst places such as **Hurley Chalk Pit** (permit only, Buckinghamshire, Berkshire and Oxfordshire Naturalists' Trust, BBONT), the **Ridgeway Path** (SU 464848–595807, Countryside Commission) and parts of **Windsor Great Park** (SU 953735) are generally accessible.

Buckinghamshire

Ivinghoe Beacon. SP 961168. 400 ha. National Trust

This large piece of Chiltern downland is rich in plants, butterflies and birds, and the views out across the Vale of Aylesbury draw large numbers of sightseers. The scrub is composed of Hawthorn, Wayfaring Tree and Whitebeam, and spreads over deep or thin grassland depending on the steepness of the slope. Salad Burnet, Common Rock-rose and Cowslip are widespread, even under areas of dense scrub, but it is the old banks that run beside the tracks where the greatest diversity of plants and butterflies can be found. Kidney and Horseshoe Vetch, Common Birds-foot Trefoil, Milkwort, Wild Thyme, Bladder Campion, Wild Mignonette, Yellow Rattle and Quaking Grass can all be found together with Common-spotted and Fragrant Orchids and small numbers of Adder's-tongue Fern. The chalkland also has Pasqueflower, Musk and the very rare Monkey Orchid. Birds include Yellowhammer, Linnet, Skylark, Partridge and Kestrel.

Others: Buttler Hangings (permit only, BBONT), Church Wood (SU 973873), Coombe Hill Nature Trail (SP 853063), Dancers' End (permit only, BBONT), Gomm Valley (permit only, BBONT), Grange Lands and Polpit Hill (SP 833045), Ridgeway Path (SP 770013–961168)

Cambridgeshire

Devil's Dyke. TL 570660–654585. 04 ha. Cambient–Cambridgeshire County Council

In the past a large portion of south Cambridgeshire was composed of open grassland grazed by flocks of domestic sheep. Today, however, the great diversity of wild plants that must have grown can be found in vestigial traces along several Saxon earthworks such as Fleam Dyke and Devil's Dyke. These archaeological relicts are the best places to see Pasqueflower, Bee and Fragrant Orchid, Common Rock-rose, Crested Bellflower and other notable rarities, such as the rare and bizarre Lizard Orchid. The habitat on the Devil's Dyke varies between an embankment thick with scrub to an open slope of downland covered in a splendid array of chalkland plants. Salad Burnet, Quaking Grass, Horseshoe Vetch, Squinancywort, Clustered Bellflower and Dropwort can all be found together with the rarer Springsedge, Purple Milk Vetch, Bloody Cranesbill and several uncommon mosses.

Others: Cherry Hinton (Limekiln Close, TL 484556), Fleam Dyke (TL 548542), Thorbourn Educational Reserve (permit only, Cambient Reserve), Roman Road (TL 494547–560498), Wandlebury (TL 493533)

Cheshire

Red Rocks Marsh. SJ 204884. 4 ha. Cheshire Conservation Trust (CCT)

It is not too unfair to say that Cheshire is not an area renowned for its grass and scrublands. However, at the north-west corner of the Wirral Red Rocks Marsh is a reserve composed of a mixture of habitats ranging between duneslacks, reedmarsh and lime-rich grassland. The dune facing the Welsh coast has Lime and Marram Grass and a typical range of open sand plants, such as Sand-sedge, Sea Sandwort, Sea Milkwort, Sea Rocket and Sea Holly, but behind these the reserve merges into a rich damp grassland where Common Birds-foot Trefoil, Quaking Grass, Kidney Vetch, Wild Asparagus, Pink Restharrow and White-flowered Danish Scurvy Grass occur with a bevy of Common-spotted and Marsh Orchid species, which have hybridised to give a wonderful variation of colour, but an impossible scope for species identification.

Others: Plumley Lime Bed (permit only, CCT), Worburtons Wood (permit only, CCT)

Cornwall and the Isles of Scilly

Again an area not renowned for its grassland. Nevertheless the Atlantic coastal cliffs have a particular type of heathland

and grassland which includes species such as Bloody Cranesbill, Salad Burnet, Fairy Flax, Heath and Pearl Dog Violet and a sub-species of Early Gentian which only occurs on the Cornish coast. Other specialities include Golden Samphire, Rock Sea-spurrey, Sea Spleenwort, Soft-leaved Sedge, Heath Pearlwort and Maidenhair Fern. Of course these plants comprise an atypical grassland which grows in the salty environments at the top of sea cliffs. The Lizard and Lower Predannack Cliffs are again an area where a peculiar type of flora occurs, but this is primarily a heathland sward formed on a serpentine-rich soil.

Cumbria

Hervey. Permit only. 100 ha. Cumbria Trust for Nature Conservation (CTNC)
This reserve is situated on a long escarpment which dips to the east and has one of its sides thickly coated with woodland. Most of the top, however, is grassland composed of Blue Moor-grass, Heather, Heath Bedstraw, Tormentil, Nat-grass and Common-bent. In the drier areas Rock-rose, Wild Thyme and Harebell grow. The pavements are fragile and there are many areas of loose scree where flat limestone slabs cover the grassland. Here Biting-stonecrop, Creeping Herb Robert, Lesser Meadow-rue, Limestone Polypodia and Rigid Buckler Fern grow as well as commoner species such as Maidenhair Spleenwort and Wall-rue. Birds include Red Grouse, Buzzard, Woodcock, Skylark, Meadow and Tree Pipit, and Black Grouse. Whilst other areas of such habitat can be found in Cumbria the area is more renowned for the Lake District National Park with all its associated mountain and moorland, their bogs and rich woodlands.

Others: Asby Scar (NY 648103), Barkbooth Lot (permit only, CTNC), Beachwood (SD 452786), Clawthorpe Fell (permit only, NCC), Moorhouse (NY 730325), South Walney (SD 215620)

Derbyshire

The Peak National Park. 140,378 ha.
Peak Park Joint Planning Board
White Peak is undoubtedly the richest wildlife area in Derbyshire and lies in the 'limestone heart' of the National Park. The grasslands here have Bloody Cranesbill, Jacob's Ladder, Globe Flower, Mossy Saxifrage and the scrub is often of Hazel, under which Columbine and Lily-of-the-valley flower. These limestone flowers contrast brilliantly with the dull moors of the dark peak, although public access to these Dales is restricted to a few footpaths. Here a mixture of cliffs, screes, grassland, scrub, woodland and the marshy banks of the many small rivers contain an extraordinary range of flora and fauna. Rusty-back Green-spleenwort, Brittle-bladder Fern and Limestone Fern occur with Nottingham Catchfly and Spring Cinquefoil. Thale Cress, Hairy Rock-cress and Narrow-leaved Bitter-cress can also be found whilst Fine-leaf and Slender Sandwort join Spring Sandwort and the Mountain Pansy. Dwarf Thistle and Tor Grass are at their northern limit here and spreads of Common Rock-rose and Kidney Vetch, Bloody Cranesbill, Lesser Meadow-rue, Carline and Musk Thistle, Marjoram, Small Scabious and Dropwort turn this whole environment into a rich botanical garden worthy of a visit from any corner of our isles.

Others: Black Rock (permit only, Derbyshire Naturalists' Trust, DNT), Cheedale (permit only, DNT), Monks Dale (SK 141725), Laffkill Dale (SK 203662), Risley Glebe (permit only, DNT), Tissington Station Cutting (permit only, DNT)

Devon

Devon is a county more renowned for the Dartmoor and Exmoor National Parks and its two separate craggy coastlines. However, at **Bury Head Country Park** (SX

943564, 46 ha, Torbay Borough Council) there is some coastal grassland, where White and Rock Stonecrop, Sea Campion, Thrift, White Rock-rose, Homewort, Goldilocks Aster, Small Hare's-ear and Small Restharrow form a unique local flora. This site is also renowned for its cliff-breeding seabirds. **Groundsham** (permit only, Devon Trust for Nature Conservation, DTNC) is an area of wet heathy grassland which is rich in meadow plants. The **Welcome and Marsland Valleys** (SX 214174, 208 ha, Royal Society for Nature Conservation) have areas of coastal turf and oak and sycamore scrub.

Dorset

Fontwell Down. Permit only. Dorset Naturalists' Trust (DNT)

Dorset is a county rich in down- and scrub-land and whilst Fontwell Down is a 58 hectare package of this environment there are many other sites as worthy of exploration. Fontwell is a dry valley, flecked with scrub and bordered with woodland on one side. Its steep slopes are filled with chalkland flowers and butterflies, amongst a scrub of Blackthorn, Hawthorn, Bramble, Gorse, Wild Rose, Dogwood, Wayfaring Tree, Whitebeam, Privet, Holly and Yew. Quaking Grass, Harebell, Carline and Dwarf Thistle, Lady's Bedstraw and Common Birds-foot Trefoil join Restharrow, Small Scabious, Wild Thyme and Salad Burnet in the extraordinarily rich chalkland flora. Less common species include Early Gentian, Clustered Bellflower, Bastard Toadflax and Autumn Lady's Tresses, and to the south of the reserve is a separate plot which is specifically managed for the benefit of a population of Greater Knapweed parasitised by Knapweed Broomrape. Other sites worthy of a visit include **Greenhill Down** (ST 792037, 12 ha, DNT), with its good numbers of Marbled White butterflies, the **Lulworth Range Walks** (SY 882804, Ministry of Defence), with their over 2,000 hectares of downland, **Powerstock Common** (SY 540963, 50 ha, DNT) with its rich bird and mammal fauna (including Sparrowhawk, Fallow, Sika and Roe Deer), **Sovell Down** (ST 992108, 1.6 ha, DNT), which has over 135 chalkland plants, and many other areas within the Isle of Purbeck's 22,000 hectares of limestone and chalk hills. Many of these are accessible because of the many footpaths and, by tramping along these, such species as Adonis, Chalkhill, Little and Common Blue butterflies, Marbled Whites, Dark-green Fritillaries, Lesser Spider Orchid, Green-winged Orchid, Buzzard, Hobby and Fallow Deer can all be found.

Others: Durlston Country Park (SZ 032773). Hod Hill (permit only, DNT), Isle of Portland (SY 682738), Townsend (SZ 025783), White Nothe Undercliff (SY 765813)

Durham, Cleveland, and Tyne and Wear

This area is more renowned for the barren moorlands of the Pennines and the beaches and cliffs of its east coast. Nevertheless there are patches of herb-rich limestone grassland. Autumn Gentian, Fairy Flax, Moonwort, Blue Moor-grass, Common Rock-rose, Northern Marsh Orchid, Pyramidal Orchid and Fragrant Orchid are among the flowers which draw a fantastic range of butterflies to **Bishop Middleham Quarry** (permit only, 9.1 ha, Durham County Conservation Trust, DCCT). A 32 hectare reserve of coastal limestone grassland can be found at **Blackhall** (permit only) and at **Gravel Hole Quarry** (permit only, 1.5 ha, Cleveland Nature Conservation Trust) there is an area of lime-loving scrub and grassland which has Small Scabious, Quaking Grass and attracts butterflies such as Small Heath and Dingy Skipper. **Trimdon Grange Quarry** (permit only, 4.8 ha, DCCT) is a scrubby limestone quarry which has Autumn Gentian, Early Purple Orchid, Cowslip, Carline Thistle and Zig-zag Clover among its flora, and Burnet Moth, Common Blue and Orange-tipped butterflies among the insects. There are numerous Yellowhammers and Willow Warblers to exploit this site, and these species can also be found at **Wingate Quarry** (NZ 373376, 22.5 ha, Durham County Council), an area where Quaking Grass, Greater Knapweed, Common Twayblade, Common Spotted and Fragrant Orchids can be found in the scrub.

Essex

Essex is an area renowned for its flat, seemingly endless and desolate shores of mud which stretch out into the North Sea. Just the other side of the Thames the rich grasslands of Kent, Surrey and Sussex stretch away from London, and any budding grassland naturalist would perhaps be best travelling around the M25 and heading south into the garden of England. However, a few sites in Essex are worthy of a visit: **Colne Valley** (TL 862296, 2.1 ha, Essex Naturalists' Trust, ENT) is a disused railway line in the process of developing into woodland. It has dense scrub, which has a bevy of warblers as breeding species. **Epping Forest** (TQ 412981, 2,438 ha, Corporation of the City of London) has a bias towards ancient woodland and thus a great diversity of flora and fauna, but it does, however, hold a few small areas of grassland, none of which stars any amazing flora or fauna specialities. **Hitchcock's Meadows** (permit only, ENT) is an area of grassy slopes which has Heath Dog Violet, Meadow Saxifrage, Green-winged Orchid, and Autumn Lady's Tresses for plant interest, a good variety of bird species and Glow-worms. **Stocking Pelham** (TL 457286, 28 ha, Central Electricity Generating Board) is an area of chalk grassland where over 60 species of birds can be found, and **Lingwood Common** (TL 783057), **Malden Wick** (permit only, ENT), **Mark's Hill** (TQ 684874), **Newland Grove** (permit only, ENT), **Nayes Point** (TM 666245) and **Skippers Island** (permit only, ENT) all have small areas of grassland and its associated flora and fauna.

Gloucestershire

Rodborough Common. SO 852035. 96.8 ha. National Trust
This level plateau of limestone grassland bears a great variety of limestone flowers characteristic of the Cotswolds. Yellow Rattle, Common-spotted Orchid, Kidney Vetch and Greater Knapweed can be found in the coarse grassland, and where the grasses grow shorter, Small Scabious, Harebell, Common Birds-foot Trefoil, Common Rock-rose, Cowslip and Eyebright join Common Milkwort and Lady's Bedstraw, Wild Thyme, Autumn Gentian, Salad Burnet, Quaking Grass and the lime-loving Hoary Plantain to enhance this astounding variety. Yellow-wort and Carline Thistle grow on the even thinner soils with Herb Robert growing on the screes themselves. In places, Bramble, Wild Rose and Hawthorn have helped Ash saplings grow into areas of scrub. Two species that have a local distribution, Pasqueflower and Wild Liquorice, join a particularly good show of orchids which include Early Purple, Green-winged, Fragrant, Pyramidal and Bee. Needless to say with such a bevy of botanical interest there is a diverse insect fauna, and a typical list of birds, including a number of warblers, Yellowhammers, Linnets and Sparrowhawks.

Others: Chedworth (SP 051138), Cooper's Hill (SO 886142), Quickly Hill Country Park (SO 936163), Elliott (SO 877067), Frocester Hill (SO 794009), Minchinhampton Common (SO 858013), Poor's Allotment (ST 559995), Snow's Farm (permit only, Gloucestershire Trust for Nature Conservation, GTNC), Stuart Fawkes (permit only, GTNC)

Greater London

Within the tangle of six and a half million people spread over one and a half thousand square kilometres there are numerous sites for any grassland naturalist to explore. At **Alexandra Park** (Wood Green, N22, 4 ha) there is a spread of some dense scrub and the former racecourse is managed as meadow grassland. At **Barnes Common** (Rock Lane, Barnes, SW13, 71 ha) there is an area of grass and scrub with a population of Burnet Rose. At **Camley Street** (St Pancras, NW1), where a former canalside coal depot has been developed into an ecological park, there is an area of grassland that supports Common Blue butterflies. **Covert Wayfield** (Hadley Wood, Enfield, 6.5 ha) has an area of tall grassland and also an area which is mown regularly to produce a herb-rich pasture. **Down Bank** (permit only, 7 ha, Kent Trust for Nature Conservation) has an area of chalk grassland which includes Toothwort and Spurge Laurel. **Hampstead Heath** (NW1 and NW3, 324 ha) has its own wild flower meadow, and the south meadow grassland and scrub which are valuable for visiting birds and insects.

Springwell Quarry (permit only, London Wildlife Trust) has Kestrels nesting on its inaccessible ledges and a flora of chalkland plants which includes Salad Burnet, Meadow Cranesbill and Fumitory. **Thames Side** (River Road, Creekmouth, Barking, 13.2 ha) is a reserve founded from wasteland on the site of the old Barking Power Station. It has Skylarks and Meadow Pipits among its grassland birds, and in winter Short-eared and Barn Owls quarter the flats looking for the resident mice and voles.

Whilst individually these areas may seem unexciting to many naturalists spoilt by the downs and scrub of southern England, for the naturalist living in the metropolis and a half a day to spare some interesting new species may only be a bus ride away.

Hampshire and the Isle of Wight

This area of central southern England joins Kent and Sussex in its richness of exceptional grassland habitats. There are many reserves, many of which have their own specialities, and in the little space available here it is difficult to do justice to any. What follows is an abbreviated list of all of those worthy of a special visit.

Broughton Down (permit only, Hampshire and Isle of Wight Naturalists' Trust, HIOWNT) is an area of fine chalk grassland which has the unusual Field Fleawort amongst its flora and Chalkhill Blue and Dark-green Fritillaries joining Ruby Tiger and Large Yellow Underwing among its insect fauna. **Compton Down** (SZ 368854, 40 ha, National Trust) is an area of downland which overlooks the sea from the south side of the Isle of Wight. Its deeper soils are filled with plants such as Cowslip, whilst its thinner soils are filled with Wild Thyme, Harebell, Quaking Grass and Yellow-wort. The summer show of chalkland flowers is exceptional. Blue-selfheal, Tiny Eyebright, clusters of Horseshoe and Kidney Vetch, Lady's Bedstraw and Squinancywort join Clustered Bellflower and Bee Orchid, Carline and Dwarf Thistle, after an earlier spread of Early Gentian, Early Purple and Green-winged Orchids. It is also an ideal site for migrant butterflies, and both Clouded Yellow and Bergers Clouded Yellow are attracted by the wealth of vetches and Adonis, Chalkhill and Little Blue are frequent. The rare and isolated Glanville Fritillary may also stray onto this reserve.

Farley Mount Country Park (SU 409293–433293, 106 ha, Hampshire County Council) is an area of chalk downland covered with characteristic plants, including the uncommon Bastard Toadflax and a bevy of Pyramidal Orchids. The associated woodland areas have rides which also contain many unusual lime-loving plants.

Martin Down (SU 058192, 249 ha, Nature Conservancy Council) has a wide range of habitat which varies from a superb mix of chalkland scrub with Ash, Buckthorn, Dogwood, Hawthorn, Privet, Spindle and Wayfaring Tree, through a small area of chalk heath and other tracts of short grazed grassland. Plants here include Chalk Milkwort, Early Gentian, Field Fleawort, Dwarf Sedge, and a variety of orchids including Bee, Fly, Frog and Burnt-tip. Insects too are quite exceptional with an outstanding array of butterflies including Adonis, Chalkhill and Little Blue, Silver-spotted Skipper, and Marsh and Duke of Burgundy Fritillaries. In the past the area was frequented by Stone Curlews, and although now these birds are largely absent, Nightingales occur in the scrub and in winter Short-eared Owls and Hen Harriers quarter this beautiful relict of English grassland. If you can sense a bias here it is not surprising. This is my favourite nature reserve in the whole of the British Isles.

At **North Hill** (permit only, HIOWNT) Yellow-wort, Autumn Gentian and Kidney Vetch attract a fine array of insects, including Marbled Whites and Duke of Burgundy Fritillaries. Orchids here include Musk and Frog. **Old Winchester Hill** (SU 647210, 60 ha, Nature Conservancy Council) is an area of chalk downland scrub and woodland which descends from the ramparts of an Iron Age hill fort. Here, Clustered Bellflower, fine spreads of Horseshoe and Kidney Vetch, Autumn Gentian and a local population of Round-headed Rampion grow amongst more common downland plants such as Hawkbits, Lady's Bedstraw, Crosswort, Eyebright and Salad Burnet. The reserve also boasts an incredible 14 orchid species. There are unusually large colonies of Fragrant, Frog and Greater-butterfly Orchid. The scrub attracts a good range of warblers and other small birds, and Kestrels and Sparrowhawks are frequently seen hunting over the reserve. Butterflies include Chalkhill Blue, Dark-green Fritillary and Duke of Burgundy Fritillary.

Oxenbourne Down (permit only,

HIOWNT) has small areas of chalk heath which are rich in birds including Blackcap, Lesser Whitethroat and Nightingale.

St. Catherine's Hill (SU 841275, 30 ha, HIOWNT) is a steep grassy knoll just outside Winchester which has a wide variety of chalkland flowers and shrubs, including Privet, Dogwood, Kidney Vetch and Rock-rose. Butterflies here include Chalkhill Blue and Marbled White.

Stockbridge Common Down (SU 377347, 89 ha, National Trust) is a long sweep of ungrazed grassland with mixed scrub and a dense scrub cover on the highest point. It provides us with a picture of Salisbury Plain before ploughing turned this into an abyss of monocultural cereals. The scrub is Hawthorn, Gorse, Blackthorn, Spindle, Privet and Dogwood, and species such as Greater Knapweed and its parasite Knapweed Broomrape grow here, as well as Lady's Bedstraw and Pale Dropwort which occur in great profusion. Birds include Kestrel, Little Owl, Skylark, Meadow Pipit, Linnet and Yellowhammer.

Others: Brook Nature Trail (SZ 391839), Catherington Down (SU 689141), Quarters Dene (permit only, HIOWNT), Micheldever Spoil Heaps (permit only, HIOWNT), Tennyson Down (SU 324855)

Hereford and Worcester

Eades and Foster Green Meadow.
Permit only. 12.2 ha. Worcestershire Nature Conservation Trust (WNCT)
Although access is only available to this site on Open Day it is still well worthy of a visit in May, when the meadow is ablaze with a spread of natural colour. Cuckoo Flower, Ragged Robin, Marsh Marigold, Cowslip, Green-winged Orchid and Adder's Tongue, join Bluebell, Bugle, Primrose, Goldilocks Buttercup, Wood Anemone and Violets in a tremendous show of an old English meadow; the woodland flowers are a relict from an old forest and the ancient hedges show how the meadow

was at some time subdivided. It has never been ploughed in living memory and that is why its grassland is so rich. After July, when the meadow is cut for hay, the short sward produces its speciality – Meadow Saffron. This species puts up its leaves in the spring to provide energy for its corm to flower in autumn. The leaves are poisonous, so grazing animals are discouraged, and although this species occurs in several woods in this part of the country this is the best surviving grassland meadow where it can be found.

Elsewhere in the area there are a series of other reserves with a grassland interest. **Boynes Coppice and Meadow** (permit only, WNCT) is an ancient ridge and furrow meadowland which has Dyer's Greenweed, Pepper Saxifrage, Adder's Tongue and Green-winged Orchid. Glowworms, Burnet Moths, Marbled White butterflies and Pale St. John's Wort can be found at **Common Hill and Monument** (permit only, Herefordshire and region Naturalists' Trust, HRNT). The **Dowared Group** (permit only, HRNT) is a collection of three reserves which have areas of grassland and scrub. Common Rock-rose, Wild Thyme, Harebell, Marjoram, Eyebright and Greater Knapweed can be found as well as Holly Blue, Pearl-bordered and Silver-washed Fritillaries and Marbled White butterflies. The scrub here also has Nightingale as a breeding species. **Long Meadow** (permit only WNCT) is an unimproved hay meadow where in spring there is a fine show of Cowslip, Green-winged Orchid and Adder's Tongue.

Others: Badgers' Hill (permit only, WNCT), Brotheridge Green (permit only, WNCT), Cother Wood (permit only, HRNT), Duke of York Meadow (SO 782354), Mowley Wood Track (permit only, HRNT), Newpenned Wood (permit only, HRNT), Pennyhill Bank (permit only, WNCT), Waseley Hill Country Park (SO 979768), White Rocks (permit only, HRNT), Windmill Hill (SP 072477)

Hertfordshire

Much of this county is founded on chalk, and the Chilterns skirt its western edge. Within this area there are small stretches of downland that remain unploughed and unimproved, but much of the grassland is now mixed with scrub through loss of grazing. Two reserves are worthy of local attention. **Blagrobe Common** (permit only, 4.3 ha, Hertfordshire and Middlesex Trust for Nature Conservation, HMTNC) is recognised as one of the richest grasslands in this region. Grazing has kept the meadow clear of scrub, and large numbers of Early, and Southern Marsh and Common Spotted Orchids can be found in early summer. Brown, Carnation, Common, Distant and Remote Sedge can be found with False-fox Sedge, Fused-flowered Spike Rush and Bristle Clubrush, Ragged Robin and Cuckoo Flower. Marsh Marigold, Lesser Spearwort and Meadowsweet, join Devilsbit Scabious and Lady's Mantle in this mixture of wet and damp areas which provide a mirror for those distant times, before farmers turned to fertilisers and herbicides. **Therfield Heath** (TL 348406, 169 ha, Hertfordshire County Council) is an area of chalk downland where Pasqueflowers still grow. In summer the slopes are covered with Milkwort, Clustered Bellflower, Wild Mignonette, Common Rock-rose, Salad Burnet, Wild Thyme, Horseshoe Vetch and Dropwort. Another local speciality, Wild Candytuft, can be found among the grasses together with Bastard Toadflax and the rare Spotted Cat's-ear. Bee and Fragrant Orchids also occur on the heaths. Bird fauna includes Skylark, Meadow Pipit, Corn Bunting, Wood and Grasshopper Warbler and Kestrel. Butterflies include Brown Argus, Common, Chalkhill and Holly Blues, Dingy, Essex, Large and Small Skippers.

Others: Alpine Meadow (permit only, HMTNC), Chorley Wood Dell (permit only, HMTNC), Hunsdon Meads (permit only, HMTNC/ENT), Patmore Heath (TL 443257)

Kent

The downlands of this area enjoy a fame which stretches worldwide, and the county's closeness to continental Europe swells its diversity of species. This influence can be seen in the plants, birds and butterfly groups, but most particularly in that of the orchids where at least five species are more abundant in Kent than anywhere else in Britain. At least twice as many more are commonly found here, especially those which are representative of chalk downland. Common Spotted, Man, Pyramidal, Fragrant, Bee, Fly, and the Spider Orchid, join Monkey, Lady and Lizard in this 'Garden of England'. Like Hampshire and Sussex good reserves are numerous and each of the following is worthy of a special visit.

Lydden Down (TR 276451, 21.2 ha, Kent Trust for Nature Conservation, KTNC) is fine chalk grassland and provides a suitable substrate for plants such as Yellowwort, Salad Burnet, Chalk Milkwort and Dropwort. Fragrant Orchid and Autumn Lady's Tresses occur amongst a bevy of Common Rock-rose, Wild Thyme, Cowslip, Dyer's Greenweed, Common Birdsfoot Trefoil, Horseshoe Vetch, Tiny Eyebright, Common Centaury, and Wild Mignonette. The downland is topped by Gorse and Hawthorn scrub which provides shelter and nest sites for all the typical downland birds, and both Marbled White and Chalkhill Blue butterflies abound. The reserve also contains a colony of the rare Wart-biter cricket. A scrub of Broom, Birch, Hawthorn, Hornbeam, Oak, Dogwood and Hazel interlaces the grasslands at **Queendown Warren** (TQ 827629, 7.2 ha, KTNC). Cowslip and Violet grow with Common Rock-rose, Wild Thyme, Marjoram, Common Milkwort and a tremendous range of orchids; Bee, Fly, Early Spider, Burnt-tip, Green-winged and Man all grow on this single reserve, making it well worthy of a visit in mid-summer. The range of habitat here also provides a suitable site for fine populations of grass-

hoppers, butterflies, and mammals, including Stoats and Weasels. The warblers are well represented and Yellowhammers, Linnets, Skylarks and Woodpeckers can also be seen. **Wye and Crundale Downs** (TR 077455, 100 ha, Nature Conservancy Council) is a large reserve having a great variety of habitats ranging from open chalk grassland through to scrub and Beech woodland. The orchids are good here, and the speciality is the Late Spider Orchid, which is possibly at its western extremity here. Early Spider, Bee, Burnt-tip, Musk and Man join the commoner Fragrant, Pyramidal and Frog on this one reserve. Within the woodland, Fly Orchid grows with that Kent speciality the Lady Orchid, and this combination of these extraordinary plants must make this reserve one of the key targets for any budding orchidophile, providing of course that he or she leaves the trowel and flowerpot at home!

Others: Denton Bank (permit only, KTNC), Folkestone Warren (TR 242373), Kemsing Down (TQ 457591), North Downs Way (TQ 428557–TR 319412), Park Gate Down (permit only, KTNC), Trowsley Country Park (TQ 634613)

Lancashire and Greater Manchester

In an area more renowned for its limestone upland and lowland mosses, mudflats and salt marshes, there are two reserves worthy of local attention. **Ainsdale Sand Dunes** (SD 290105, 492.5 ha, Nature Conservancy Council) is a huge area of coastal sand dunes and extensive dune slacks where a specific type of grassland is encouraged by the lime-rich sand. Plants such as Early Marsh Orchid, the beautiful Marsh Helleborine, Kidney Vetch, Yellow-wort and Autumn Gentian can all be found, but the specialities of the reserve include Grass of Parnassus, Round-leaved Wintergreen and the rare and elusive Dune and Pendulous Helleborines. A wide variety of insects and birds can also be found, and the scattered pinewoods contain a population of Red Squirrels, something to brighten any botanical foray. A similar habitat can be found at Lytham St. Annes (ST 309307, 16 ha, Lytham Borough Council) where a sward of rolling Marram and finer grasses spread over lime-rich shell sand. Typical plants include Yellow Rattle, Kidney Vetch, Wild Pansy, Carline Thistle, Biting Stonecrop and Yellow-wort. More exciting however, is the Evening Primrose which grows in the moist dune slacks. The insect life includes White-satin, Cinnabar and Burnet Moths, Grayling, Common Blue, Green-veined White and Small Copper butterflies, five species of bumble bee and a variety of unusual ladybirds.

Others: Ainsdale and Birkdale Hill (ST 298127), Cheadle Hulme (SJ 875855)

Leicestershire and Rutland

Cribb's Meadow. Permit only. 4 ha. Leicestershire and Rutland Trust for Nature Conservation (LRTNC)
In an area not famed for any rolling downland, extensive machair or valleys of scrub, this reserve nevertheless represents a valuable history of old grasslands. It is composed of two fields on either side of a scrub-covered railway line, both of which are unimproved old meadows, full of flowers such as Cowslip, Green-winged Orchid, Buttercup, Common Birds-foot Trefoil, Lady's Bedstraw, Yellow Rattle, Great Burnet, Adder's Tongue, Pepper Saxifrage and Common Spotted Orchid. The scrub is composed of Wild Rose, Hawthorn, Blackthorn, Crab Apple and Dogwood, and along the railway line Kidney Vetch, Ox-eye Daisy, Herb Robert, and Perforate St. John's Wort can be found, as can Common Blues and Small Copper butterflies. The scrub is also a useful cover and breeding site for warblers and the ubiquitous Yellowhammers. A similar reserve can be found at **Wymondham Rough** (permit only, LRTNC), and here the

specialities include Beautiful Dropwort, and Harvest Mouse.

Others: Ambion Wood and Shenton Cutting (permit only, LRTNC), Bloody Oaks Quarry (permit only, LRTNC), Brown Hill Quarry (permit only, LRTNC), King Lud's Entrenchments (permit only, LRTNC), Miles Heath (permit only, LRTNC)

Lincolnshire and South Humberside

Several reserves in this area show a wide variety of grassland types. The extensive dunes and marshes of **Gibraltar Point** (TF 556581, 428 ha, Lincolnshire and South Humberside Trust for Nature Conservation, LSHTNC) contain swards of Sand Couch and Marram and ridges of Sea Buckthorn. Mosses, lichens, Ragwort, Hound's-tongue and Birds-foot Trefoil grow as well as Cowslip, Lady's Bedstraw and the Pyramidal Orchid, but really the reserve is more known for its coastal attributes. However, **Redhill** (TF 264807, 3.8 ha, LSHTNC–Leicestershire County Council, LCC) is a chalk grassland reserve, half of which is situated in an old quarry. It is full of lime loving plants, including Kidney Vetch, Yellow-wort, Bee and Pyramidal Orchid, Basil, Thyme and Autumn Gentian. Beyond the hill the chalk grassland has developed into a scrub, but the open downland attracts a range of butterflies, including Common Blue and Meadow Brown. Birds include Meadow Pipit and Yellowhammer. The site is also of geological interest. **Snipe Dales** (RF 320863, 48 ha, LCC–LSHTNC) is a long grassland valley speckled with stands of Hawthorn, gorse and Great Willow-herb. Common Spotted Orchids can be found as well as eleven different butterfly species. The omnipresent Linnet and Yellowhammer join Meadow Pipit, Reed Bunting and a range of six species of breeding warblers including that horrific skulker, the Grasshopper Warbler. Both Short-eared and Barn Owls hunt over the area.

Others: Axholme Lime (SK 773997),
Candlesby Hill Quarry (permit only,
LSHTNC), Fir Hill Quarry (permit only,
LSHTNC), Furze Hill (permit only,
L3HTNC), Heath's Meadow (permit
only, LSHTNC), Little Scrubb's
Meadow (permit only, LSHTNC), Mill
Hill Quarry (permit only, LSHTNC),
Moor Closes (permit only, LSHTNC),
Rush Furlong (permit only, LSHTNC),
Swayby Valley (permit only, LSHTNC)

Norfolk

Whilst Norfolk is one of Britain's natural
oases and a site for many naturalists' pil-
grimages, its grasslands are mainly grassy
heaths and have been outlined in the
Heathland book of this series. Grassy
heaths worthy of visit include: **East
Wretham Heath** (TL 914886, 147 ha,
Norfolk Naturalists' Trust, NNT) where a
large number of lime-loving species can
be found in the tangles of Wavy Hair-grass,
Ling and the scrub of Broom and Hawthorn. Birds include Skylark, Nightingale,
Grasshopper Warbler, Whinchat,
Wheatear and Nightjar. At **Weeting Heath**
(permit only, NNT–Nature Conservancy
Council) many characteristic Breckland
plants such as Early Forget-me-not, Rue-
leaved Saxifrage, and Spiked Speedwell
join a range of butterflies including the
Essex Skipper and Holly Blue. This
reserve is most frequently visited, however, because the observation hides allow
superb views of the increasingly rare
Stone Curlew during the summer months.
Norfolk also has a chalk downland reserve
at **Ringstead Downs** (TF 706400, 10.5
ha, NNT) where a public track runs through
a dry valley filled with lime-loving plants
such as Rock-rose, Squinancywort, and
Wild Thyme. There is also a good range of
birds and butterflies.

Others: Blakeney Point (TG 001464, NNT),
Chedgrave Common (TM 372993),
Holkham (TF 892447, NCC), Roydon
Common (permit only, NNT)

Northamptonshire and the Soke of Peterborough

Barnack Hill and Holes. TF 075046. 22
ha. Nature Conservancy Council –
Northamptonshire Trust for Nature
Conservation, NTNC
The hills and holes of this reserve were
excavated by medieval craftsmen who
used the stone and rubble to build the
great cathedrals and abbeys of
Peterborough, Ely, and Bury St Edmunds.
Once abandoned, a short turf colonised
the rubble and this remained until the First
World War when scrub encroachment
began to damage the site. Under management the scrub of Turkey Oak, and Hawthorn has been controlled and a splendid
range of limestone-loving flowers has
been encouraged. Cowslip, Quaking
Grass, Small Scabious, Dropwort, Common Rock-rose, Horseshoe Vetch, Purple
Milk Vetch and Squinancywort are all common, whilst spikes of the parasitic
Knapweed Broomrape and a range of
orchids provide extra interest. These
include Bee, Fragrant, Pyramidal and the
increasingly rare Man Orchid. However,
pride of botanical place goes to the very
restricted Pasqueflower – that beautiful
silky violet relict of old downland.

Others: Castor Hanglands (TF 118023), Colly
Weston Quarry (permit only, NTNC),
Denford Churchyard (permit only,
NTNC), Glapthorn Cow Pasture
(permit only, NTNC), Irchester
Country Park (SP 912658), Ramsden
Corner Plantation (permit only,
NTNC), Walton Grounds (permit only,
NNT)

Northumberland

Northumberland is known for the Cheviots
and the associated Northumberland
National Park, and also for its offshore
islands, such as Lindisfarne and the Farne
Islands. Whilst grasslands here are ubiquitous in terms of high moorlands or dune

slacks the range of grass- and scrub-lands covered in this book are only represented by a number of small reserves worthy of a local visit. **Barrasford Nick** (permit only, Northumberland Wildlife Trust, NWT) is composed of two quarries filled with Crested Hair-grass, Hare's-foot Clover, Wild Onion, Dyer's Greenweed, Common Rock-rose, Fairy Flax, Restharrow, Small Scabious and Cup-leaved, Long-stalked and Woods Cranesbill. Huge old spoil heaps thick with scrub and lime-loving plants, such as Quaking Grass and Fairy Flax, can be found at **Black Pasture Quarry** (permit only, NWT) whilst at **Cocklawburn Dunes** (NU 032482, 6 ha) a coastal sward includes Cowslip, Bloody Cranesbill, Autumn Gentian, Purple Milk Vetch and Kidney Vetch. Although **Flodden Quarry** (permit only, NWT) is primarily a geological exhibit its grassland holds species such as Doves-foot Cranesbill, Common Storksbill, Polypody, and a fine range of mosses, liverworts and lichens. **Little Mill** (permit only, NWT) another disused quarry has a range of pond, scrub and grasslands which supports Fairy Flax, Wild Carrot and typical scrub birds such as Whitethroat, Yellowhammer and Willow Warbler.

Others: Arnold (NU 255197), Crindledykes (permit only, NWT), Lowick Quarry (permit only, NWT)

Nottinghamshire

Clarborough. Permit only.
Nottinghamshire Trust for Nature
Conservation (NTNC)
This long, narrow, 5 hectare site holds a range of habitat; short turf, where typical plants of downland can be found such as Common Birds-foot Trefoil, Cowslip, Common Centaury, Common Milkwort, Bee Orchid, Hoary Plantain, and Yellow-wort, long grass, where species which can tolerate the competition and shade such as Ox-eye Daisy, Spiny Restharrow, Hairy St John's Wort, Pyramidal and Common Spotted Orchids grow. Where the grass is thicker still Wild Rose, Privet, Dogwood and Hawthorn soon grow into established scrub woodland, where Elder, Field Maple and Sycamore cover Sanicle, Woodruff and sheets of Ivy. Such a range of habitat attracts a typical range of scrub birds, including many warblers and also a fair variety of butterflies.

Others: Bentinck Bank (permit only, NTNC), Eakring Meadows (permit only, NTNC), Fairham Brook (SK 562338), Farnsfield–Southwell Nature Trail (SK 675566–643573), Kimberley Cutting (permit only, NTNC), Lady Leigh Quarry (permit only, NTNC), West Burton Meadow (permit only, NTNC), Wilwell Farm Cuttings (permit only, NTNC)

Oxfordshire

Aston Rowant. SP 741967. 124 ha.
Nature Conservancy Council
This magnificent example of Chiltern scarpland is at a glance what English grassland is all about. Within the reserve there is a small area of chalkheath, where acid-loving plants such as Heather, and Heath Bedstraw are mixed with lime-loving species in a sward which is tightly grazed and contains many typical downland plants, such as Sheep's Fescue, Glaucous Sedge, Salad Burnet, Common Rock-rose, Wild Thyme, Eyebright, Common Milkwort, Quaking Grass, Horseshoe Vetch, Birds-foot Trefoil, Common Centaury, Ox-eye Daisy, Marjoram, Wild Mignonette, Common Spotted Orchid, Squinancywort, Yellow-wort and Kidney Vetch – the list is almost endless. The scrub is formed of Dogwood, Privet, Hawthorn, Elder, Whitebeam and Yew. This is also a fine site for Juniper scrub and probably is the most northerly representation of this habitat in Britain. The woodland which tops the reserve is worthy of a visit, because both White and Violet Helleborine can be found on the bare floor under the

Beech canopy. Good populations of Dingy and Grizzled Skipper, Chalkhill Blue, Brown Argus, Green Hairstreak, Dark-green Fritillary and Duke of Burgundy Fritillary occur. Of outstanding interest however is the Silver-spotted Skipper, a species limited to our southern chalk grasslands. A typical scrub bird fauna can be found, with Fallow and Muntjac deer, Badger, Fox, Stoat, Weasel and Harvest Mouse forming the mammalian contingent.

Others: Chinnor Hill (SP 766002), Hook Norton Railway Cutting (permit only, BBONT), Otmoor Rifle Range (permit only, BBONT), Warburg (SU 720880)

Shropshire

In the land locked county of Shropshire much of the natural habitat is dominated by the highland influence-of the Welsh massif, a focal point for geologists who come to study ten out of twelve recognised geological ages in this one area. There are two reserves worthy of special grassland interest.

Earl's Hill (SJ 409048, 40 ha, Shropshire Trust for Nature Conservation) is a 315 metre high steep-sided bluff, which was once an Iron Age hillfort. Scrub is now returning to much of the open pasture and, whilst the summit and slopes are still mainly grass, the reserve has become a complex of habitats ranging from open rock scree through to established woodland. Navalwort and Woodsedge can be found on the scree, with Bracken, Bramble, Bluebell, Lesser Celandine and Primrose along the edge of the Ash scrub which is invading the grassland. There is a rich birdlife which includes woodland species, such as Pied Flycatcher, Redstart and Wood Warbler, whilst raptors such as Sparrowhawk, Kestrel, Buzzard and Merlin can be seen from the hill-top. Twenty-nine species of butterflies have been recorded including Silver-washed and Dark-green Fritillary, Dingy, Grizzled, Large and

Small Skipper and Holly Blue.

The other reserve worthy of a local visit is **Llanymynech Rock** (SJ 266218, 2.4 ha, Shropshire Trust for Nature Conservation–Montgomery Trust for Nature Conservation). This disused limestone quarry has a belt of woodland grading into scrub and a spread of grassland and scree. Ox-eye Daisy, Common Birds-foot Trefoil, vetches, clovers, Blue Milkwort, Marjoram, Wild Thyme, Rock-rose and Yellow-wort form the botanical interest whilst a fine array of butterflies join the usual bird species.

Others: Llynclys Common (SJ 273237)

Staffordshire

Allimore Green Common. Permit only. 2.5 ha. Staffordshire Nature Conservation Trust (SNCT)

This small site of unimproved pasture is ablaze with wild flowers in summer. Meadowsweet, Hemp Agrimony, Marsh Marigold and later Ragged Robin, Greater Birds-foot Trefoil, Marsh Bedstraw, Devilsbit Scabious and Knapweed form a mat over the meadow grasses, rushes and sedges. Marsh and Common Spotted Orchids and Water Mint join Marsh Pennywort and Grass of Parnassus amongst the scrub which provides shelter and nest sites for a typical range of scrubland birds. The **Manifold Valley** (SK 100543, 7 km, National Trust–Staffordshire County Council) has a footpath which runs through areas of grassland as well as along a river bank and through wooded slopes and cliff screes. Salad Burnet, Eyebright, Harebell, Lady's Mantle and Marjoram join Small Scabious, Wild Rose, Rock-rose, Quaking Grass and Common Spotted Orchid. Some of the lower meadows are also rich in herbs such as Devilsbit Scabious, Ox-eye Daisy and the delicate and pretty Green-winged Orchid. A fine range of warblers visits in summer to breed and the ornithological interest is increased by the presence of

Dippers and Kingfishers along the rivers.
Others: Mottey Meadows (permit only, NCC),
          Ward's Quarry (permit only, SNCT)

Suffolk

The grasslands of Suffolk, known as the brecklands, have been included in the Heathlands book of this series. Sites such as **Cavenham Heath** (TL 757727), **Dunwich Common** (TM 476685), **Thetford Heath** (permit only, NCC–Norfolk Naturalists' Trust, NNT) and **Wangford Glebe** (permit only, Suffolk Wildlife Trust, SWT) have been outlined in the book of that title. However, several other grassland reserves are available for a local visit. The **Fox Fritillary Meadow** (permit only, 2.4 ha, SWT), the best East Anglian fritillary meadow, is open one day a year, generally in early May, to show a superb array of these beautiful and now isolated flowers. The Open Day is advertised in the local press and National Botanical journals and a visit is well worthwhile to see these extraordinary plants in a density of a quarter of a million plants per hectare. **Gromford Meadow** (permit only, 1.7 ha, SWT) is a wet peaty area which supports Adder's Tongue, Marsh Valerian, Yellow Rattle, Bogbean, Marsh Marigold and Water Plantain, but the local speciality is Grass of Parnassus which is growing at the southern end of its range here. **Lady's Mantle Meadow** (permit only, 3.6 ha, SWT) has a great variety of plants, including Cowslip, Restharrow, Pepper Saxifrage, together with orchids that include Twayblade, Common Spotted, Early Purple and Green-winged, and **Mickfield Meadow** (permit only, 1.8 ha, SWT) is another, smaller, fritillary meadow which under management has increased in ecological value.
Others: Martin's Meadows (permit only,
          STNC), North Warren (TM 455587),
          Westleton Heath (permit only, NCC)

Surrey

Close to the heart of southern England, Surrey is an area which enjoys the chalk hills of the Weald and the North Downs. Hence open chalk downland is typical of its landscape, and combined with Wiltshire, Hampshire, Sussex and Kent this is one of the most valuable areas to be explored by the grassland naturalist. Whilst valuable footpaths meander through the farmland there are relatively few grassland reserves. However, the following are worthy of visit.

Boxhill Country Park (TQ 179513, 253 ha, National Trust) is not strictly a nature reserve and unfortunately suffers other public recreational pressures. Nevertheless the Box and Yew woods here provide an insight into this community. The slopes below this woodland range from scrubby to open and here Wild Rose, Marjoram, Milkwort, Salad Burnet, Horseshoe and Kidney Vetch and Sainfoin join Stinking Hellebore, Ploughman's Spikenard, and Man Orchid. Other orchids include Autumn Lady's Tresses, Bee, Musk, Pyramidal and Fragrant. The large and edible Roman Snail is common here and numerous butterfly species include Chalkhill Blue and Silver-spotted Skipper, both southern grassland specialities. The herb-rich grassland of **Headley Warren** (permit only, 31.2 ha, Surrey Trust for Nature Conservation, STNC) is gilded by a matrix of species that includes Cowslip, Common Rock-rose, vetches, Yellow Rattle, Yellow-wort, Milkwort, Chalk Milkwort, Small Scabious, Clustered Bellflower, Marjoram, Restharrow and Basil Thyme. The whole area is alive with butterflies and bees in summer. Indeed 35 species of butterfly have been identified, including the striking Adonis Blue, Duke of Burgundy Fritillary, and migrant Clouded Yellows. As usual an array of grassland birds such as Whitethroat, Yellowhammer, Linnet and Partridge can be seen.
Others: Bookham Commons Nature Walk (TQ
          121567), Epsom Common Nature

Trail (TQ 196609), Hackhurst Down (TQ 096486), Northdown Way (SU 844467–TQ 429561), Seale Chalk Pits (permit only, STNC)

Sussex

This is a county dominated by the wondrous Weald and the chalkhills of the South Downs which rise dramatically from the English Channel and swing inland and westwards to the Hampshire border. Despite the decline of sheep-farming, which maintained these downs, and the loss of much of this pasture to arable land, the area remains comparatively rich in chalk grassland habitat. Apart from the **South Downs Way** (SU 762193–TV 600972) which runs for 129 kilometres from the Hampshire border to the coast at Beachy Head, there are a number of reserves worthy of visit.

At the **Beachy Head Nature Trail** (TV 586956, 2 km, Eastbourne Borough Council) five species of blue butterfly can be found skimming over the Kidney Vetch and Wayfaring Tree, whilst the warm and sheltered reserve at **Castle Hill** (TQ 367074, 45 ha, Nature Conservancy Council) has Dropwort, Yellow-wort and Small Scabious for botanical interest, and Corn Bunting, Meadow Pipit, Skylark, Linnet, Whitethroat, and Yellowhammer for birdwatchers to enjoy. **Cuckmere Haven** (TV 519995, 392 ha, East Sussex County Council–Lewes District Council) is a huge area of chalk grassland which has variations of short and tall species-rich swards and different densities of scrub. Early Purple, Pyramidal and Common Spotted Orchids grow along with Autumn Gentian, Salad Burnet, Common Centaury, Carline and Dwarf Thistles, and in the deeper grassland, Wild Carrot, Wild Mignonette, Viper's Bugloss, Yellow Rattle and Red Bartsia thrive. The reserve runs down to the sea, where three of the Seven Sisters chalk-cliffs lie within the country park, and all the variety of coastal clifflands can be

enjoyed. At **Kingley Vale** (SU 824008, 114.4 ha, Nature Conservancy Council) there is one of the finest Yew woodlands in Europe. This is spread over the steep chalk slopes where spreads of scrub and chalk heath join in a complex mosaic of grassland, filled with lime-loving species. Eleven orchid species have been recorded here, including Fly, Bee, Frog, Fragrant, Pyramidal and Autumn Lady's Tresses. There are four blues, five fritillaries and five skipper butterfly species together with Glowworms and a great array of beetles.

Others: Ditchling Beacon (TQ 329133), Duncton Chalkpit (SU 961162), Levin Down (SU 886134), Lullington Heath (TQ 545018), Seaford Head (TV 505980)

Warwickshire and the West Midlands

This is an area of intensity. Intense industry in the Black Country and intense agriculture in Warwickshire. Mixed with this complex of modern development there is a scattering of areas rich in wildlife and there are three reserves worthy of local visit.

Draycote Meadows (permit only, 5.2 ha, Warwickshire Nature Conservation Trust, WARNACT) is two small fields which have retained their diversity of flowers in this age of improved grassland. They are rich in Cowslips, Green-winged Orchid, Adder's Tongue, Feathery Pignut, Yellow Rattle and the unusual Moonwort fern. Common Birds-foot Trefoil, Selfheal, Agrimony and Spiny Restharrow also grow, and a small area of Gorse and Hawthorn scrub can be explored, although this area is strictly managed to maintain the species-rich herbage.

Harbury Spoil Bank (permit only, 2.4 ha, WARNACT) is a lime-rich grassland which has grown on spoil from a railway cutting. Here Carline Thistle, Yellow-wort and Quaking Grass as well as Little Blue, Marbled White, and White-letter Hairstreak butterflies provide the interest, whilst at **Oxhouse Farm** (permit only, 7.2

ha, WARNACT) the rich limestone ridge is often smothered with Travellers' Joy, which engulfs and envelops the shrubs and trees which grow along the old railway line. Lime-loving plants here include Wild Basil, Salad Burnet, Dyer's Greenweed, Carline Thistle, Quaking Grass, Small Scabious, Greater Knapweed and the spectacular Woolly Thistle. Thirty species of butterfly have been identified including Dark-green Fritillaries, Marbled Whites and Green Hairstreaks. Scrubland birds include Nightingale, Willow Warbler and Yellowhammer.

Others: Draycote Water Country Park (SP 467692), Hartshill Hayes Country Park (SP 315945), Stockton Railway Cutting (permit only, WARNACT), Ufton Fields (permit only, WARNACT)

Wiltshire

Whilst Wiltshire to many means Stonehenge, Avebury and Salisbury Cathedral, it also means Salisbury Plain and the Marlborough Downs. These two distinct areas constitute two thirds of Wiltshire and here the chalk downland can contain up to 40 plant species per square metre, including a dozen species of orchid and many other attractive flowers. As ever the downland is under threat by scrub invasion and ploughing but several key reserves exist and are worthy of a special visit.

Lavington Hill (permit only, 9.2 ha, Wiltshire Trust for Nature Conservation, WTNC) is particularly rich in plant species because of the shallow soil on its slopes. Yellow Rattle, Greater Knapweed, vetches, Tiny Eyebright, Agrimony, Birds-foot Trefoil, Lady's Bedstraw, Cowslip, Ragwort, Yellow-wort, Common Centaury, Restharrow, Squinancywort, and Clustered Bellflower produce an extended blaze of colour throughout the spring and summer seasons. These species are joined by Bee and Pyramidal Orchid, Star-of-Bethlehem and the ever spectacular Woolly Thistle. Marsh Fritillary, Chalkhill Blue and Green

Hairstreak provide the lepidopteran interest. At **North Meadow** (SU 099944, 39 ha, Nature Conservancy Council) a great variety of meadow plants grow. Adder's Tongue, Great Burnet, Cowslip, Ox-eye Daisy, Southern Marsh Orchid, Common Meadow-rue join the most extraordinary show of fritillaries in the country. At this one site in spring you can see perhaps 80 per cent of the total British population and this is well worthy of a visit from any corner of our Isles. The almost legendary **Pewsey Downs** (SU 115635, 166 ha, Nature Conservancy Council) is to me what old downland is all about. It is composed of a huge sward of Red and Sheep's Fescue Grasses with Glaucous Sedge, Salad Burnet, Dwarf Thistle, Tor Grass and an exciting array of orchids. These include Burnt-tip, Common Spotted, Bee, Frog, Fragrant and Pyramidal. The curious Knapweed Broomrape grows here as a parasite on Greater Knapweed, and other uncommon species include Roundheaded Campion, Early Gentian, and a hybrid between Dwarf and Tuberous Thistles. The wealth of plants supports a wide range of insects including Brown Argus, Chalkhill and Little Blue, and Marsh Fritillary. Single species aside, it is the spectacular view out over Salisbury Plain which makes this such a valuable reminder of how important these few remaining relicts of our grassland really are.

Others: Barbury Country Park (SU 157761), Ilen Down (permit only, WTNC), Hetley Hill (permit only, WTNC), Pepperbox Hill (SU 212248), Prescombe Down (permit only, NCC), Ridgeway Path (SU 118681–259833 CC), Upper Waterhay (permit only, WTNC), White Sheet Hill (permit only, WTNC), Wylye Down (SU 002363)

Yorkshire and North Humberside

In an area dominated by the North York Moors National Park and the Yorkshire Dales National Park, there are nevertheless a few grassland reserves worthy of local visit. **Ashbury** (permit only, 5.3 ha, Yorkshire Wildlife Trust, YWT) has a good range of limestone plants including Bird's-eye Primrose, Globe Flower and Grass of Parnassus. **Kipling Cotes Chalk Hill** (permit only, 4.4 ha, YWT) is a small area of chalk grassland and scrub where Red and White Bladder Campion, Wild Thyme, Germander Speedwell, Wild Pansy, Lady's Bedstraw, Cowslip, Quaking Grass, Common Spotted and Pyramidal Orchid join Ox-eye Daisy, Kidney and Tufted Vetch and Hop Trefoil. Butterflies include Large Skipper, Ringlet, Meadow Brown, Small Heath, Dingy Skipper and Common Blue. The typical range of scrubland birds can be found.

Others: Bempton Cliffs (TA 197738), Brockadale (permit only, YWT), Malham Tarn (SD 890672), Maltby Low Common (permit only, YWT), Wharram Quarry (permit only, YWT)

WALES

Clwyd

Graig Fawr. SJ 064802. 24.6 ha.
National Trust

This reserve is situated on a limestone hill. The western and northern faces are steep whilst the eastern and southern parts slope more gently. Here there is a shallow turf which is full of small herbs and lime-loving plants such as Wild Thyme, Small Scabious, Lady's Bedstraw, Common Birds-foot Trefoil, Hoary Rock-rose, Biting Stonecrop, Carline Thistle and Salad Burnet. A similar flora can be found at **Loggerhead's Country Park** (SJ 198626, 27 ha, Clwyd County Council) where a grassland plateau has these species with others such as Bloody Cranesbill, Harebell, Common Milkwort and Eyebright. Paths lower on the cliff faces are edged with the immigrant Rose of Sharon.

Others: Bishop's Wood Nature Trail (SJ 068813), Bryn Euryn Nature Trail (SH 834802), Ddôl Uchaf (permit only, North Wales Naturalists' Trust)

Dyfed

Dyfed is an area starved of any specific grassland reserves. For the naturalist here it is the dramatic sea coast and its associated clifftop flora and fauna which are of outstanding interest. These areas including those offshore islands in the Scomer complex, have been described and outlined in the Rocky Shorelands book in this series. However grasslands of a type can be encountered over many parts of the Pembrokeshire National Park where 270 kilometres of coastline can be explored. In other areas there are dune slacks, and their associated grassland, which are worthy of exploration and at **Llyn Eiddwen** (SN 606674, 48 ha, West Wales Naturalists' Trust, WWNT) there is an upland lake with some associated grassland. At **Nant Melin** (permit only, 2.8 ha, WWNT) there are some wet grasslands adjoining woods where plants such as horsetail, Royal Fern and Globe Flower can be seen, but if any West Wales naturalist is sufficiently keen to see distinct grassland fauna he should fuel his car and drive eastwards along the M4 and into the heart of southern England.

Glamorgan

Glamorgan is not a county renowned for its grassland reserves. However three are worthy of a visit if you are in the area: **Lavernock Point** (permit only, 5.8 ha, Glamorgan Naturalists' Trust, GNT) is a coastal area covered with dense Hawthorn scrub on a bed of limestone grassland. Here Adder's Tongue and several orchids, including Lesser Butterfly, Green-winged and Bee Orchid, can be found. Many warblers, Linnets and Yellowhammers can be found in the tangle of scrub. **Llanrhidian Hill** (SS 497922, 3.1 ha, GNT) is composed of two quarry sites where Elder,

Hawthorn and Ash scrub mix with some limestone grassland to provide an interesting habitat with its associated variety of plant and insect life. Linnets, Stonechats, Yellowhammers and Whitethroats can all be found here, but perhaps Glamorgan's best grassland reserve is at **Ogmore Down** (SS 897762, 26.5 ha, GNT). Here, squashed between several quarries, is an area of limestone grassland where Lady's Bedstraw, Common Birds-foot Trefoil, Common Centaury, Eyebright, Wild Thyme, Small Scabious, Salad Burnet, Harebell and Autumn Lady's Tresses can be seen along with a rare sub-species of Hairy Violet, and a peculiar Horseshoe Vetch. There is also an area of limestone heath, where normally acid-loving plants, such as Gorse, Ling and Bell Heather grow alongside more typical limestone species, such as Common Rock-rose and patches of scrub provide ideal nesting habitat for Skylark, Stonechat and Yellowhammer. Glow-worms are of particular local interest.

Others: Bunkers Hill (permit only, GNT), Cosmeston Lakes Country Park (ST 180693)

Gwent

Ysgyryd Fawr SO 330180 83 ha
National Trust
This reserve is situated on a hill which rises clear of some farmland and is an outlier of the Black Mountains. On the lower slopes there is an area of Bracken, Gorse and Foxglove, intermingled with scrub of Hawthorn, Ash, Birch, Crab Apple and Oak, but above this, towards the 486 metre summit, there are large areas where rough grassland forms grassy plateaux of Bilberry, Wild Thyme and Harebell. Mosses and lichens abound on the fallen scree and Hart's Tongue Fern can be found amongst the damper escarpments. Birds include Linnet, Stonechat and Sparrowhawk.

Gwynedd

The Nature Reserves in Gwynedd are dominated by upland and woodland types. At **Bryn Pydew** (permit only, 5 ha, North Wales Naturalists' Trust, NWNT) there is an area of limestone pavement and limestone grassland where plants such as Rock-rose, Bloody Cranesbill, Lily-of-the-valley and the extraordinary Dark Red Helleborine can be seen, along with Brown Argus and Dingy Skipper butterflies and the occasional Glow-worm. At **Cors Goch** (permit only, 46 ha, NWNT) there are areas of damp fen and grassland which hold Grass of Parnassus, Early and Northern Marsh Orchid, Common Spotted Orchid and Marsh Helleborine, all of which are locally uncommon. On the drier areas Rock-rose, Fairy Flax, Salad Burnet and Quaking Grass can be found, and over 600 species of insect have been identified on the reserve including 250 moths and butterflies. Birds include that scurrilous skulker the Grasshopper Warbler, heard if not seen, and other wet-loving species such as Reed Buntings, Lapwings, Redshanks and Snipe. At **Gogarth** (permit only, 2 ha, NWNT) there is an area of limestone grassland and scree where many typical plants, such as White Hoarhound, Wild Madder and Hoary Rock-rose, can be found along with dwarfed forms of Grayling and Silver-studded Blue butterflies. The rare Hoarhound Plume Moth which can otherwise only be found in southern England also occurs.

Others: Cors Tyddyn Du (permit only, NWNT), Nantporth (permit only, NWNT)

Powys

Lake Vyrnwy SH 985215 6,500 ha
Royal Society for the Protection of Birds
It is difficult to classify this reserve simply as a grassland area because it is composed of a flooded valley surrounded by conifers, broad-leaved trees, and great

spreads of moorland which form part of the largest heather moor in Wales. However some grass, moor and old meadow pastures increase the habitat range, and patches of thick scrub provide nesting habitat for Pied and Spotted Flycatchers, Redstart, Wood Warbler, Tree Pipit and Whinchat. On the grassland, Harebell, Sheep'sbit Scabious, Heath Bedstraw, Betony, Welsh Poppy and Golden Rod can be found. Powys is an area forming the backbone of Wales and is primarily composed of upland, moorland or woodland reserves, and any local Welsh naturalist with a bent for the exploration of grassland should take a trip to southern England to explore the habitats there.

Others: Craig Irfon (permit only, Brecknock Naturalists' Trust), Llandeilo–Graban Roadside (SO 090438–SO 112419)

SCOTLAND

Borders

St. Abb's Head. NT 9168. 97 ha.
National Trust for Scotland, Scottish Wildlife Trust
There is no doubt that this is a seabird colony reserve, complete with spectacular scenery and a rich marine life – the ten thousand or more Guillemots, Kittiwakes, Razorbill and Fulmars are of prime importance – yet within the Borders it is the only reserve which encompasses anything like a habitat defined as grassland. Behind the cliffs there are areas of short tufted grassland which descend through a series of humps and hollows down to a loch in the valley bottom. Here Common Rock-rose, Birds-foot Trefoil, Thyme, Thrift and Sandwort can be found with Tormentil, Milkwort and a scrub of wind-bent Hawthorns and Sycamore.

Central

Go south, bonnie Scots, go south!

Dumfries and Galloway

South, Jimmy, south!

Fife

Jimmy – I said south, now spin your sporran and travel!

Grampian

You take the high road and I'll take the low road, and I'll be in Wiltshire afore ye!

Highland North

A rough calculation shows that Cape Wrath and Dunnet Head are the two sites on the British mainland that are furthest away from the Late Spider Orchids in Kent!

Talic. Permit only. 13.5 ha. Scottish Wildlife Trust
This site has some dry pasture that is believed never to have been ploughed and consequently holds a wide range of herbs including Fragrant, Early Purple and Lesser Butterfly Orchids.

Lothian

Abberlady Bay. NT 4681. 582 ha.
East Lothian District Council
Famed for its birds this area also has a botanical interest and some dune scrub and grassland. Here mosses and lichens, Autumn Gentian, Grass of Parnassus, Burnet Rose and Moonwort can be found with Early Marsh and Northern Marsh Orchids, with 15 species of sedge growing in the slacks.

Outer Hebrides

This area has extensive tracts of a peculiar

type of grassland known as machair. Because of its sandy seaside association this habitat will be dealt with in a forthcoming tome entitled Sandy and Muddy Shores.

Strathclyde South

Auchalton Meadow. Permit only. 4 ha. Scottish Wildlife Trust
This area of lime-rich grassland is worthy of a visit from mid-June to July when the wide variety of herbs and grasses are at their best. Adder's Tongue, Common Twayblade, Greater, Lesser Butterfly and Frog Orchid, Field Gentian and Quaking Grass are among the more exciting of the 98 plant species that have been identified on this small reserve. However, over 140 species of herbs and grasses have been counted at **Feoch Meadow** (permit only, 10 ha, Scottish Wildlife Trust) which is a site of ancient meadowland situated on lime-rich rock. Here the orchids include Fragrant, Frog, Small White, Greater and Lesser Butterfly. There are 14 species of butterflies recorded including the very local Large Skipper.

Tayside

Brerachan. Permit only. 0.5 ha. Scottish Wildlife Trust
Between May and July this tiny uncultivated meadow is worthy of a visit to see Globe Flower, Spignel, Melancholy Thistle and Quaking Grass, which occur among the 119 plant species recorded in this last vestige of a former hay meadow. At **Keltneyburn** (permit only, 31 ha, Scottish Wildlife Trust) there is a comparatively lime-rich soil which supports Greater Butterfly, Frog, Small White and Fragrant Orchid as well as Field Gentian, Globe Flower, Spignel, Burnt Saxifrage and the Moonwort Fern.

SOME USEFUL ADDRESSES

Alpine Garden Society
Lye End Link
St. Johns
Woking
Surrey GU21 1SW

Amateur Entomologists Society
355 Hounslow Road
Hanworth

The Botanic Society of the British Isles
c/o Natural History Museum
Cromwell Road
London SW7 5BD

British Butterfly Conservation Society
Tudor House
Quorn
Nr. Loughborough
Leicestershire LE12 8AD

British Trust for Ornithology
Beech Grove
Tring
Hertfordshire HP23 5NR

Conservation Association of Botanical Societies
323 Norwood Road
London SE24 9AQ

The Mammal Society
Burlington House
Piccadilly
London W1V 0LQ

National Council for Conservation of Plants & Gardens
c/o Wisley Garden
Woking
Surrey GU23 6QB

Nature Conservancy Council
Northminster House
Peterborough PE1 1UA

Orchid Society of Great Britain
c/o L. E. Bowen
28 Felday Road
Lewisham
London SE8 7HJ

Royal Entomological Society of London
41 Queens Gate
South Kensington
London SW7

Royal Society for Nature Conservation
The Green
Nettleham
Lincoln LN2 2NR

Royal Society for the Protection of Birds
The Lodge
Sandy
Bedfordshire SG19 2DL

Wild Flower Society
Harvest House
62 London Road
Reading
Berkshire RG1 5BS

BIBLIOGRAPHY

Belmann, H. *A Field Guide to the Grasshoppers and Crickets of Britain and Europe.* Collins, London, 1987.

Bunn, D. S., Warburton, A. B. and **Wilson, R. D. S.** *The Barn Owl.* T. & A. D. Poyser, Calton, England, 1982.

Carter, D. *Butterflies and Moths in Britain and Europe.* Pan, London, 1982.

Carter, D. J. and **Hargreaves, B.** *A Field Guide to the Caterpillars of Butterflies and Moths in Britain and Europe.* Collins, London, 1986.

Chinery, M. *A Field Guide to the Insects of Britain and Northern Europe.* Collins, London, 1979.

Corbet, G. B. and **Southern, H. N.** (Eds) *The Handbook of British Mammals.* Blackwell Scientific Publications, London, England, 1977.

Cramp, S. and **Simmons, K. E. L.** (Eds) *A Handbook of the Birds of Europe, the Middle East and North Africa. The Birds of the Western Palearctic.* Vols. I–IV. Oxford University Press, England, 1977.

Davies, J., Davies, P. and **Huxley, A.** *Wild Orchids of Britain and Europe.* Chatto & Windus, London, 1983.

Evans, G. (Ed) *The Observer's Book of Birds' Eggs.* Frederick Warne, London, 1972.

Fabre, J. H. and **Black, D.** (Eds) *Insects.* Nature Classics, Paul Elek, London, 1979.

Ford, E. B. *Butterflies.* New Naturalist, Collins, London, 1945.

Fuller, R. J. *Bird Habitats in Britain.* T. & A. D. Poyser, Calton, England, 1982.

Garrard, I. and **Streeter, D.** *The Wild Flowers of the British Isles.* Macmillan, London, 1983.

Hayman, P. *The Birdwatchers Pocket Guide.* Mitchell Beazley, in association with the Royal Society for the Protection of Birds, London, 1979.

Harrison, C. *A Field Guide to the Nest Eggs and Nestlings of British and European Birds.* Collins, London, 1975.

Harrison Matthews, L. *Mammals in the British Isles.* New Naturalist, Collins, London, 1982.

Heinzel, H., Fitter, R. and **Parslow, J.** *The Birds of Britain and Europe with North Africa and the Middle East.* Collins, London, 1972.

Hubbard, C. E. *Grasses, a Guide to their Structure, Identification, Uses and Distribution in the British Isles.* Penguin, Harmondsworth, England, 1954.

Hugh Newman, L. *Looking at Butterflies.* Collins, London, 1977.

Hywel-Davies, J. and **Thom, V.** (Eds) *A Guide to Britain's Nature Reserves.* Macmillan, London, 1984.

Jones, D. *The Countrylife Guide to Spiders of Britain and Northern Europe.* Hamlyn, Feltham, England, 1983.

Kerney, M. P. and **Cameron, R. A. D.** *A Field Guide to the Land Snails of Britain and North Western Europe.* Collins, London, 1979.

Knight, C. and **Brooks, M.** *A Complete Guide to British Butterflies.* Johnathan Cape, London, 1982.

Krebs, J. R. and **Davies, N. B.** *An Introduction to Behavioural Ecology.* Blackwell Scientific Publications, London, 1987.

Lack, P. (Ed) *The Atlas of Wintering Birds in Britain and Ireland.* T. & A. D. Poyser, Calton, England, 1986.

Lang, D. *Orchids of Britain.* Oxford University Press, England, 1980.

Langer, R. H. M. *How Grasses Grow.* The Institute of Biology, Studies in Biology Number 34. Edward Arnold, London, 1979.

Linssen, E. F. *Beetles of the British Isles.* Frederick Warne, London, 1959.

Lloyd, H. G. *The Red Fox.* B. T. Batsford, London, 1980.

Lousley, J. E. *Wild Flowers of Chalk and Limestone.* New Naturalist, Collins, London, 1950.

Lockley, R. M. *The Private Life of the Rabbit.* André Deutsch, London, 1965.

McClintock, D. and **Fitter, R. S. R.** *Pocket Guide to Wild Flowers.* Collins, London, 1974.

McNeill Alexander, R. *The Invertebrates.* Cambridge University Press, 1979.

Moore, I. *Grass and Grasslands.* New Naturalist, Collins, London, 1966.

Nilsson, S. and **Mossberg, B.** *Orchids of Northern Europe.* Penguin, Harmondsworth, England, 1979.

Peterson, R., Mountfort, G. and **Hollom, P. A. D.** *A Field Guide to the Birds of Britain and Europe.* Collins, London, 1983.

Phillips, R. *Wild Flowers of Britain.* Pan, London, 1977.

Putman, R. J. and **Wratten, S. D.** *Principles of Ecology.* Croom Helm, Beckenham, England, 1984.

Ragge, D. R. *Grasshoppers, Crickets and Cockroaches of the British Isles.* Frederick Warne, London, 1965.

Reade, W. and **Hosking, E.** *Nesting Birds, Eggs and Fledglings in Colour.* Blandford Press, London, 1967.

Salisbury, Sir E. *Downs and Dunes, Their Plant Life and its Environment.* G. Bell, London, 1952.

Sharrock, J. T. R. (Ed) *The Atlas of Breeding Birds in Britain and Ireland.* T. & A. D. Poyser, Calton, England, 1976.

Simms, E. *British Thrushes.* New Naturalist, Collins, London, 1978.

Smith, C. J. *Ecology of the English Chalk.* Academic Press, London, 1980.

Tansley, A. G. *Britain's Green Mantle; Past, Present and Future.* George Allen and Unwin, London, 1949.

Whalley, P. *Butterfly Watching.* Severn House Naturalists' Library, London, 1980.

LOOKING AFTER GRASSLAND

Our heathlands are always under serious threat from fire because they are naturally a parched habitat. Grasslands too can become extremely dry in high summer and dry rank grass is superb tinder. Consequently care should be taken when discarding cigarettes, even when using wastebins. If you smoke be sure to extinguish your cigarettes fully. Do not light fires and be vigilant of other peoples' negligence. Report fires to the Fire Brigade immediately, however small. If fire beaters are available do your best to safely control the fire until the Brigade arrives.

Litter is a secondary problem. Not only does it aesthetically scar any habitat, it can be harmful to the species which live there. Take it all home with you. Drink cans, their pull rings, beer grips, plastic bags, bottles and paper can all be killers when investigated or ingested by our fauna. Mammals are especially at risk. If you don't love it, don't use it. If you love it, don't lose it.

THE PHOTOGRAPHS

All the photographs in this book were taken using 35 mm Canon SLR cameras A-1 and F-1 in conjunction with the following Canon FD lenses; 28 mm, 50 mm, 70–210 mm zoom, 100 mm macro and 500 mm F8 reflex. They were all taken using Kodachrome 64 slide film using a tripod and cable release. In some cases filters have been used, primarily 81B, Softner and polarising, to enhance or destroy some aspect of the reality.

Figures in bold type refer to photographs
(often with text on same page); figures in
italics refer to colour paintings.

RIGHT **A piece of history**

123